Intrusive Thoughts

Eric Krueger

PublishAmerica
Baltimore

First printing

At the specific preference of the author, PublishAmerica allowed this work to remain exactly as the author intended, verbatim, without editorial input.

ISBN: 1-4137-9134-4
PUBLISHED BY PUBLISHAMERICA, LLLP
www.publishamerica.com
Baltimore

Printed in the United States of America

A WISE MAN ONCE SAID

A wise man once said:

Come all, come all

The tart apples that make us ponder of life

The smooth texture that is so sweet

Light pours out its innocent brilliance upon thy self

Sculptor of what we call life, stands fast as marble statues

The baritone notes that lay in ones deaf ear

A WISE MAN ONCE SAID

HOPE

A new day blooms about, from the shadows of yesterday

New life springs about, cast the old away, beginning a new day

I walk the sandy shores of such youth, glazing at the vast ocean of impend-
ing waves

Tainted with the condition of love, encompassing all that live

I hold your hand, conveying my unconditional love for you

For you complete me, fitting the missing link to the ultimate puzzle

We watch the sun rise, pouring its brilliance upon us all

Life giver, breathes fresh air into our lungs, filling them up with the very
meaning of life

The caged bird is now set free, unleashing its compassion for the world

For the caged bird now sings the sweet melodies of the silent symphony

Only to soar above the white dove clouds, freedom rings about

Life, a vivid experience to ones mind, intrusive thoughts race through my
mind

Conveying both truth and purpose, the very definition of life itself

Such wisdom that springs onto the flowers of empathy, foreshadowing a
new beginning to an old end

For no spell cast sorrow on us, for we are free, free to live, free to be

How sweet life is, how grand it can be

To forever set one's man soul to thee, Creator in all, so ever divine, a
thousand thanks to you, and also to mine

WISE

A wise man once said:

The tart apples that we ponder of life

The smooth texture of what it brings to bay

Light pours out its innocent brilliance upon thy youthful self

Sculptor of what we call life, stands fast as marble statues

The baritone notes that lie in ones deaf ear

A wise man once said

A WOUND

A wound so deep that no bandage could repair

A wound that cries for love

Cast a spell, a thousand years ago, stirring new memoirs of today

Stirring vivid thoughts and intense emotions

Emotions that can not be seen, nor heard, but felt within thy inner heart

Intrusive thoughts of lust intrude thy mind, restless as can be,

Cannot sleep, pacing around the house again and again

Searching for some sort of salvation, but where to be found?

Searching for some cure, a cure to make the restless sleep

Need to relax my mind, ease up on the gas pedal

Slow Down! Take a breath, come to my senses!

This wound is far beyond repair, for it is bruised black and blue

Only solution, to treat it with love, for love heals all

Slowly, but surely, it gets better, new life springs about

For in times of darkness, I see only but light!

INNOCENT CHILD

A young child sits about, mixing the solution to eternal love

For it can not be seen, nor heard, but felt within thy inner layering of one's heart

Beating rhythms of liquid peace, that pours through out our veins, ever so cold

The innocent child, fears nothing, for he does not know even the meaning of fear

His eyes glaze into mine, our hands meet, in which, intertwine

To taste such youth, to feel that young, this is where life, just had begun

His tiny hands, stir the mixture, creating a paste of infinite joy

The fields are then spread, from within all the little boys

Hearing melodies, that derive so deep, for only the deaf can hear, the
constant beat

So young, so innocent, such love that pours about, this child's life, is never
at fault

To hold him ever so tight, the mighty grasp from within, such compassion
lays, in which to begin

Thy only love, forever the day will stay, switching forth hate and dismay

MY LOVE TO YOU, EVER SO STRONG, THIS INFINITE KISS,
THAT WE MAY

NEVER MISS, FOR I AM TO YOU AS YOU TO I, WE SOAR EVER,
SO VERY HIGH

ALL ALONE

Constantly risking absurdity, I stare into your ever so glazing eyes

For whenever she performs, I stare without any hesitation

Thinking of you, I pace the pits of fire

Beauty stands alone and waits

This is my salvation

Constant phases of the moon

Casts a spell, confusing thy mind

Loveliest of all trees, you are the light in darkness, pouring out such youth

Where is thy innocence, why does it stay? For what does it convey?

Naked to thy very body, my soul, ever so strong

The imprisonment of such intrusive thoughts, unanswered questions of the mind

Smoky rain, riddles the vast lake, deceitful waves of impending doubt

The orchard of artificial light, leads but in the wrong direction

Summer by day, winter by night

Plains of hope, seem to grow, springing new life about

Maturing sun, pours out such passion

A winnowing wind, only heard by the deaf

Barred clouds clutter the sky, shedding its pain and sorrow

LIFE, HOW LONELY CAN IT BE

GOD'S INNER MIND

Amongst the mountain, one walks the valley of death

To smell the unfolding anger, opens up as a distant novel

Opening the pages, comes with full force, with no remorse,

For the lovers that may be

Slowly walking upon the cliffs of fear, all I see, is death in thy mirror

Summertime vines running down my spine, forever tickling one's soul

Currents of life, look how they flow

Step by step, taking his time

Balancing on life's, thin cable line

I offer you a hand, to be lead

Through the thick and thin

A flower so dead

The very essence of life, lays in thy single kiss

Number one, on the grocery list

In the green trees shadow, in this I lay

Protecting me from, brother sun, his brilliant ray

Take this time, to read each and every rhyme

For unlocking the puzzle, of God's inner mind

AMONGST THE STARS

True love, its own personality

Flows deep within your veins

As a fish needs water, so does love

For love is a vast ocean, never ending, open to all directions

Love, such impending wave cast about, imprinting our feet in the moist sand

Leaving or own mark, to know that this was our moment

Pink-vanilla sky, shedding drip lets of rain

Cleansing thyself, naked to thy eye, free

We dance amongst the stars, parade about, skipping on each other

How life is so grand!!

For the greatest thing in life to love and to be loved

FREEDOM

Amongst the white fields and beyond, I slept

I slept, as if time didn't exist, in which everything stood still

A thousand souls stir in the nights, though, being me, I slept

Such vivid happiness abound, though still, I slept

As if life were just a dream, and all realities were phony, in a sense, fake

And then one lonely day, **I WOKE UP**

Such a glorious day that it was!!

To hear the birds chirping, the wind whispering, the sun and it's unconditional warmth

Oh, such a life that may be!!

To smell the unfolding beauty that lies about, so innocent, without a fault

To dance and parade amongst the yellow glazed stars!

Such a life, for now I am but alive

In essence, now I LIVE

OPEN TO THEE

An old man once said:

Make yourself into light?

For life is too dark as we know it!

Make yourself experience life, not to just live it!

As the man inhaled his final breath, he let out a sigh

And finally saying-the greatest thing in life is to love and to be loved

For this is the very essence that the white dove sings, its melodies in all

All day I think of you, wordless, perfect love

Prevailing in the darkness, a light, is reunited

For aren't we all but human beings? To live and to experience!! In such, so divine!!

For we complete each others hunger

To be one again

ANXIETY

Comes in full force, giving the need, for it to proceed

Thunder strikes from the heavens above, foreshadowing the day to come

For it is still young, and its elders have not woken up set

Heart beast a thousand times a second, grasping for the needed air

For that is the very meaning of life, such air to breathe

Life giver, hold on tight, for the storm is just now acting up

Calm by day, fierce by night, impending waves parade along side the vast
shore, our feet imprinted there, leaving our territory mark

Legs start to go numb, loose, wiggly to thy tender most touch

Breathless about, grasping thy lungs, such air is know where to be seen

Restless as can be, taking one more step would not seem wise

Pacing about, with intrusive thoughts, are they my fault?

For what have I done? What is thy case?

Do I deserve this as my elder neighbor?

Suddenly the thoughts seem to wash away, as water sweeping back into
the lake

A DREAM PER SE, A DREAM!!

LIFE'S PLEASURES

Around the world, here we go, passengers of the train of life

Traveling amongst the hidden stars, breathing in such life, it's beautiful melodies

Float amongst the clouds, feather of life, such meaning you bring to me

Caged bird now set free, shinning with ultimate glee

Brother sun, show us the way, to the golden palaces above, home of the elders

They say that they play chess, each move, independent of the other, taking the vivid steps of life, pondering about

Scribbling freedom, painting bright emotions, confirms one's intrusive thoughts

For black and white has no meaning nor place in here

For in death, I see only but life, life that springs from the pebbles and seeds

Forming one's body, mind, soul, ever so complete

Walking amongst sister moon, setting the mood for tonight, we are but one again

You show me the very meaning of life, to love and to be loved

For one needs not to live, but to **EXPERINCE,** such vivid emotions that hold ever so true

Canvas of life, paint me something good today, show me the essence of love

I'M NO ANGEL, BUT I DO KNOW HOW TO SMILE

I still know how to fly, to soar ever so high, enlighten the pink vanilla sky

So this is what it is like to be human

AH, LIFE, HOW GRAND CAN IT BE

OUR GARDEN

As a leaf that blooms, becoming united in youth

Becoming of age, turning night into day, turning darkness into light

A leaf that is ever so healthy, shedding rain drip lets of innocence on the
naked ground

Feeding the soil such passion, a vast blanket of water soothing the ground

For new life grow amongst here, springing about, to become alive again

As a flower, pedals of love me, love me not, are blown in the wind

Carrying the scent of freedom, sun glaring it's age upon us all

Sister moon is a sleep, not feeling so well

A garden, such a garden, to walk in the inner realm

Where all of life exists, vivid pleasure runs down thy spine

Life, isn't it ever so grand, a garden of love, creating nothing into something

Creating the unknown to the known

THIS IS OUR GARDEN, SO DO NOT TREAD ON IT

CHILD

Child, that lays in such content, pleasure abound

Pondering life, its purpose in all

How beautiful it is, what dreams may come

Child, that rests upon my naked arms, I see the world in you, such vivid colors that you paint

Child, that cries through the late night, do not worry, for the night is young, and day is almost here to stay

Child, that smiles throughout the day, yes, I know, isn't life grand!!

Child, that runs from room to room, slow down, take life moment by moment, for we know that life is too short already

Child, that becomes a teenager, brush your teeth, pull up your baggy pants, and give thanks to those who care

Child, now 21, an adult, it is time now for you to discover the world, grasp it!

Live life without a doubt! Stay young! Seize the moment! You will live longer

For it is now time for me to go, I have another life waiting in the heavens above

One day we will meet again, but until then, a thousand kisses and hugs

COLD SUMMER RAIN

Cold summer rain, shedding it's youth upon us all

Casting away deceitful sorrows, stirring new memoirs for the day

A new beginning to an old end, for young life springs about

From the stems and roots of thy inner soul

Brother sun, sister moon, show us the way to the golden palace

One in which we can taste the foreign fruits, such a pilgrimage it may be

Landing on the sandy shores, shedding away our innocence, for we are
whole again

Imprinting our feet, setting our mark in this place that we call life

For the vast ocean have no boundaries, swimming afar

Each stroke, independent of each other, representing life's steps toward

A new level, one in which scribbling freedom amongst the pink-vanilla sky

Shinning through the pale grey clouds, leading us into the right direction

Casting a spell of such ecstasy, many more to come, to save this day

For this is our day, our moment in time, in which we too belong

Invitations dart amongst the rain, cleansing thy body

A new beginning to an old end

A single feather floats amongst us, conveying the very meaning of life

How we too float upon the riptides of life, such currents flowing about

Without a doubt, I love you, from the moment I set thy naked eyes upon

Your love, mine, together, we intertwine

Our hearts beat the rhythm of the marching band

You make me feel so young again, forever we are to be

To set the caged bird free, to soar to ever new heights, new levels of existence

COMING HOME

FLOATING HOME WITH THESE VIVID OCEAN DREAMS,

COMES THY SWEET SCENT OF STRAWBERRIES

KISSING THY LIPS

UNLOCKING THE KEY TO A FLOATING DREAM

WISE WORDS

A wise man once said:

The tart apples that we ponder of life

The smooth texture of what it brings to bay

Light pours out its innocent brilliance upon thy youthful self

Sculptor of what we call life, stands fast as marble statues

The baritone notes that lie in ones deaf ear

A wise man once said

FAMILY PRIDE

Father, forgive me, for the spell of doubt, cast about

I love thee with all my might, to battle from within,

Round three, fight!!

For you are the world to me, your universe sets the white heavens free

Freedom glistens upon my soul, my elaborate body, filled with love so content

In all, too divine, one breath, one touch, one love

You complete me, as I to you

With all my soul and heart, may our bond never depart

For watching stars without you, my soul cries

I NOW SET THE CAGED BIRD FREE, FOREVER TO LIVE, IT'S BEAUTIFUL

LIFE, ONCE AGAIN THEE

CAGED BIRD

Death, is it nothing more than a word?

Is death the darkness in which one sleeps through at night?

What is death, for what does it convey? What is thy message?

Is death the lonely night that passes us by?

Is death the middle of a cold winter day?

Is it but the freezing rain that darts upon us?

Is death the dark room in which one sleeps upon at night?

For in darkness, I only see light!

For in death, I only see life!

What death do you talk about?

What death do you convey?

For there is no death in me, for I am forever set free!

There is no death in my meaning of life, for there is only life, to live amongst the stars, to be forever free

SWEET MELODIES

Do we know of thy music that we make?

Do we hear the silent symphony too?

For aren't we the ones to play such vivid tunes?

Do we know of the rain that we make?

Such thunderstorms that lay about, spreading as a white sheet amongst the green-bladed grass

Do we know of such wind that we make?

The ones that fill our very lungs with the essence of life,

Do we know that we are life givers, not takers?

What do we really know?

To thee, I know this much, for without love, there is no logic, for one is constantly lost

The greatest thing in life is to love and to be loved, for this, I DO KNOW

MY PALACE

This is my domain, of which I speak of thee

God's golden palace, soon, to replace me

To hear the vast melodies, that spring about

To feel such passion, without a single doubt

To become one again, soaring so vividly in the sky

This untouchable addiction, ah, feeling so high

To taste the bitter-sweet symphony

ONCE AGAIN, TO BECOME THEE

FEAR AWAITS

Fashion tinted robes of sorrow

Cleanse my eyes, fields of fire conveying, little star

Swimming into a swift, rapid ghastly river of fear

To float and flow, water encompassing one's true soul

Such wanderers in this sad, deceitful valley of hope

Where to go? What to do? Which direction heads upon north?

When will we reach the golden doors of the palace?

Our spirits moving, musically through the currents and tides of life

What time shall death cast upon?

A vast parade of ghostly echos simmer through our veins

For each breath, now breathless about

Where to go? What to do?

GOD FORGIVE THOSE WHO DOUBT, FOR IT ISN'T BUT THEIR
FAULT

THOUGHTS OF PLEASURE

Glimmer thoughts race through my mind, my heart beats the rhythm, in all,
so divine

I can hardly breathe, for my lungs are full, could this be real, oh no

My vision blurs ten times worse, death has cast a spell, a wicked curse

I watch and see, my legs wobble about, I am not doing this, how then is it
my fault

What death shall I meet, wherever I go, the imprints of my feet

For if I go, tell yourself never to let go, for in darkness shines light, we
shall win this fight, if ever, were the ones who are right!!

What mysteries life brings, little pebbles, glowing as diamond rings, for
this is our marriage

And this shall be our own carriage, of love so strong, a double sided band
aid, holds such the bound

We walk along the shores of the distant sea, soaring as high, being so free,
the very bird that sings our names, at our heart he aims

For the greatest thing in life, is to love, and to be loved, to the white dove
clouds, which we fly above

Mark this day, mark this moment, forever it stays

The directions to love, head north this way

I kiss thy hand, with my inner most soul, together we shine, together we flow

As water, drip lets on the side, never, never to subside

POET'S COFFEE

He drinks five cups of coffee in the morning

Adds a touch of milk, two spoonfuls of sugar

Trying to rid that early morning hangover, one that consumes all

He scans through the newspaper, hardly able to concentrate, he lights up a cigarette

Breathing in so deep, one said that he smokes poetry in his dreams

Hardly scanning the words written, he thinks about the night before, oh, how it ever was!!

Such memoirs that stirred throughout the day, though, he can hardly recalls what took place

Standing in the cold kitchen, he pours new water and food for his two dogs

Another day, just breathe he says, everything will be alright!?

The darkness of yesterday now subsides away, for today is a new beginning to an old end

The sun now shines its beauty upon thee, pouring out its brilliance

Such knowledge one obtains just from looking at the sun, revelations abound

For the past is the past, and the future is the future, but now, at this very moment, life begins to take place!!

SWEET SURRENDER

Hearing ones laughter stirs the memoirs of a new day

Laughter, bringing joy to the everlasting family

Laughter, bringing us one step closer, each step creates a new stride

Laughter, singing melodies of youth, dancing amongst the hidden campfire

Laughter, holding hands with each other, becoming one again, reunited

Laughter, filling our lungs with such sweet air, tickling our bodies

Laughter, making us skip and parade about, with no one at fault

Laughter, a silver coin in a thousand gold pennies, naked to the human eye

Laughter, a cure for the common cold, as if it were chicken noodle soup

Such warmth, such taste, the sun dancing amongst the tongue

To never take life too seriously, laughter is the very meaning of life

HER LOVELY DRESS

Her new dress, shown in darkness, had a tinted glow to it

For it fit perfectly on the little girl, shinning another days pure brilliance

For in this very darkness, there was nothing but light, truth in all

In this darkness, lay a thousand souls, lost, trying to find way

In this darkness, directions confused and lost, hidden path unknown to thy naked eye

In this darkness, the little girl shed her sweet tasting innocence, an invitation to a select few

In this darkness, lays no death, but life, unconditionally, to the last breath

Her new dress, shown in darkness, encased no such fear, for what is the meaning of it

Glowing star of life, life giver, not taker

FOR YOU ARE THE VERY MEANING OF LIFE

RESTLESS MIND

How beautiful is her unshakeable sleep!!

Her elaborate body, lying so content, so love abound

Her eyes, shut from the outer world, dreams of fantasies, of what to be

Her mind, so vivid, intrusive thoughts pour out their brilliance upon thee

Setting forth new memoirs of the day, forever, forever, to stay

I was just minding my own business, when suddenly, she awoke!!

Such a glorious day to be, setting ones soul ever so free!!

Her heart, mine, together they intertwine, amongst the grapes of wrath

Such new, selected love, subsides between the two of us, two peas in a
pod, together, fullness, one being

Volume one, the new book awaits to be opened and read

Innocent tears to be shed, upon thee

For I have heard this tune before, foreshadowing of what to come

Shall we dance, we shall celebrate this golden day, may it always stay, in
thy true moment

**AND HENCE FORTH, WE DANCED, AMONGST THE STARS,
FOREVER**

**BEHOLDING THEM, TOGETHER OUR SOULS CRY, SCRIB-
BLING**

FREEDOM IN THY AIR

DO WE SPEAK OF SUCH LOVE?

I am in love, in which I speak of truth and honesty. I always tell myself
that I

love thee, with no hesitation, I soar amongst the white dove clouds, jeering
nothing but

glee. I soar ever so high, that one cannot see with the naked eye. But
instead to feel

within thy inner heart. I will convey truth, honesty, and above all, respect.
I am one, one

being, complete with my crisp vivid senses that take me afar, to the infinite
fields of love.

To run about, holding hands with one another, so free we are, no limits
cast upon us, I

see your true colours, painted about, on the canvas of life. I see right
through to you, and

such a glorious day it shall be. One taste, One touch, One love. That your
world is my

world, and shall we live together. I glaze into your eyes, scribbling free-
dom about

, becoming whole again. As water, flowing through our veins, we ride the
impending

currents to such afar. I kiss thy tender lips, conveying my love to you, without any

hesitation. I have nothing but love for you, for I will always love you, with the inner most

heart. This is where the new beginning starts and the old end stops. You and I, well, we

grasp the mighty world, blowing it as if it were dust in thy mighty hand. We walk

amongst the sandy shores, imprinting our feet, making our statement of love. For they

share remain there forever. And in the night, we shall swim, gliding through the lucid

water as if we were two fish in the sea. We sing songs of joy, jeering one's mind about.

Your stroke, independent of mine, two peas in a pod. This is what life is about, to love

and to be loved in return. The next day returns, and I shall wake up gazing upon my

beautiful wife, never to let go. For she breathes life into me, filling my lungs up with full

compassion. Without you, I am nothing, but a tiny spec in the night. I shine only when

you are beholding me. Ecstasy then runs down my spine, ah, how can such a feeling be.

A high in all, too divine to describe, black and white has no meaning here. For this is my

domain. There is no more grey zone about, for it is not our fault that it exists. I run my

hands down your back, caressing the soothing skin that lays about. In the morning, we

head off to the dog races. We bet on all, and we win!! What a delight it is. I stare into

your face, seeing such unfolding beauty, for your eyes shine with glee. I kiss thy tender

hand, conveying my soul to you. The day is young, and night has not set shown it's

face. We walk at our own pace, skipping and striding about. I see the vast lake upon us,

and decide to take a swim. The water seems so young, so alive with brilliance. As if I am

one with you, drip lets on the side, but one, human being against another. I swim out far

past the dock, swimming each stride with the intent to never stop. I am now in the middle

of this vast sea, toddling about, tasting the sun amongst my tongue. Tell me, how does it feel?

Warmth is now rested upon my body, a blanket of security, protecting me from the deceitful sorrows. I can see you on the peer, but why do you not want to come in? Why

is thee so opposed? What have I done wrong? Tell me so!! And in the presence of the

waves tumbling over and over, she walks away. What is the meaning of this? She is now

out of sight, and a thousand souls stir in the night. Where is thy love now? Where has it

gone? I swim back in, with vast content, pondering a million questions in my mind. She

just left, without no sign or signal. Sorrow pours upon my body now, and thy stomach

seems so empty. My legs tremble with fear, my body shakes and trembles. My only love

from my only hate, for today is too soon, and tomorrow is too late!! The weather now

seems to get darkened. Grey clouds hence come about, thunder strikes at bay. Tiny drip

lets of a forgotten love come about. They dart down as if it were to strike one dead. It is

now over, between you and I. For the love that we had, was a false story in all. As life is

the way it is, first is thought, then is action. And this is how the story of love ended.

ANGEL HIGH ABOVE

I'm no angel, but I do know how to smile

I'm no angel, but I still can try

I'm no angel, but I still can fly

I'm no angel, but I can still give a kiss

Where you are is where I want to be, setting one's soul, ever so free

I'm no angel, but I still know how to love

I'm no angel, but I do know how to be loved in return

I'm no angel, but I can still soar, above the white-dove clouds

I'm no angel, but I still can show you the way, to the golden palaces above

Where the elders speak and play their game of chess

Each move, independent, comes with full force

With no remorse, forgive those who do not stand by your side

For I am no angel, but I do know how to be human!!

Where you are is where I want to be!!

ESSENCE OF LOVE

I believe that you lead a happy life

I believe that life's deceitful sorrows were captured by the morning glory

I believe that there was no robe of tinted darkness stretched upon thee

I believe that there was no bitter-sweet symphony playing it's melodies

I believe that you did taste the foreign fruits of your endless pilgrimage

I believe that you did swim under the waterfall, and cleanse thyself of hate

I believe that you did run through the infinite cornfields with your hands
spread in the air, an invitation in all

Yes, I do believe that you lead a happy life, for this is all that I convey,
nothing more, nothing less

I believe that you always were at your best

**I believe that you did not live life, but, in essence, experienced it, for
all eternity**

I AM SORRY THAT I LET GO

I could never have let go

For this wound was too deep, to hard to close

You complete me, as a single blade of grass, I blow into the air

I could have never let go

For without you, I couldn't breathe, grasping for air

I need not lie down, even though I am very tired

The bandages fit ever so well, closing the gap of sorrow

We leave tidemarks from the vast lake, imprinting our feet

Making our stand, always to stay the course

I could have never let go

For you complete me, making me feel young again, scribbling youthful-
ness in the vivid air

Soaring ever so high, the pink-vanilla sky, awaits our being

Today, I miss you ever so much, a dying heart that becomes

I AM SORRY THAT I LET GO

TAKEN ON A JOURNEY
OF MEMOIRS

I have to say, life is hard, it consists of a journey
For the memoirs of yesterday just seem to fade away
One might question, what is the meaning of all this?
What does it convey?
I say to you, life, is taking steps to a never-ending marble staircase
Each step, independent of each other, battles the truth and honesty
Of each and every human being, for we are all here, aren't we
If thyself is true, as so to you, I will always be there by your side
To stare into the pitch black abyss, that lies so deep,
Take my hand, no, grasp my hand, for we are to embark on an infinite journey
Through the thick, green, bladed grass of youthfulness, we stand side by side
And open our arms to the heavenly skies above, blow a sweet virgin kiss
Amongst the blind mist, for true love can not be seen, nor heard, but felt in
thy tender heart
Freedom runs down our spines, conveying the true essence of life, its
purpose in all
They say that when you die, all your questions to life are answered, what,
hold on a minute
From the moment I wrote this poem I knew the answer, To connect and
only to connect
FOR LIFE IS TO LOVE AND TO BE LOVED IN RETURN
Without this, there is no logic
So for all those who ponder so much, may you breathe life, and let life live
for you

BECOMING ONE AGAIN

I lay on the musty floor, shackled from head to toe

For life has a grasp of one-hundred fold

I stare into the abyss, in which direction I lay

Smelling the innocent strawberries of life, that encompasses my soul,
blankets thy tender heart

To stare, without any hesitation, proudly lifting my head up high

Though my heart is cut into two, one of pleasure, and one of pain

To taste the bitter sweet blood, that swims through my veins

Hearing the silent symphony, the marching of one-thousand souls

An invitation foreshadowing of what may be

A dinner of foreign fruits, to taste the unfolding beauty of ones soul

To see the canvas of life, painted so brilliantly, vivid colours in all

To touch the songs of thy heart, that play its lucid memoirs

To be one again, as water, you complete my melodies

PEACEFUL SLEEP

I lay thee down to sleep

To watch over with glazing eyes

To make sure that you are ever so content

To make sure that my very love is meant

To know that one is to be ever safe

To know now and believe in thy faith

I love you, for you are the world to me

Your love, your passion, sets one's spirit free

The heavens above pouring its brilliance upon thee

For you make up, an innocent piece of me

Sleep thy tender child, sleep with ease

To taste inner love, to ever so please

MOTHERLAND

I look into the mirror

Ask me what I see

I see death

A reflection at best

Soon to die, just like the rest

A sad soul, that lays so near

An emotion felt, with such intense fear

In this I pray, to the elders high above

Wishing, wishing God, to let me soar amongst the white dove

Such happiness it brings

Clouds of love, show us the way

Passing life's toll, 2 dollars I must pay

Watching life go bye, for the car travels fast

Distant memoirs, are all but the past

For three things that I must convey, one taste, one touch, one love,

From the elders high above

Grasp the wind, with thy mighty hands

God, o God, take us to the motherlands

MEMOIRS OF AN ANGEL

I may not be an angel, but I do know how to smile, I do to know how to live

Tell me that I can't win, and I shall do it over and over again

Tell me not to fly, and I will soar above the white dove clouds, ever so high, scribbling freedom in thy air

All day it rained, and we danced amongst the yellow glazed skies, of no such boundaries

There we were, nothing between us, one being, complete, all encompassing

Just the simple clouds flying as kites above our elaborate bodies

So high there were, amongst the golden palace of the elders, spreading such melodies about

The winds high pitched voice, shouting invitations to come and play, for this is our day

The very meaning of today, the caged bird is hence set free, free as can be

To soar to new heights, in which the naked eye cannot see

For there is nothing for us, but love and to be loved

This very essence of life itself, to stand erect as a marble statue, without any hesitation

Standing tall as can be, such power, such strength

I now know why the caged bird sings, it's melodies in all, never to fall

LONELY PLANET

I once was absent from this world, for I lived in a different one

For 18 years had gone by, forever sleeping the day away

I have now just woken up, smelling the unfolding beauty that lies about

I once was absent from this world, for I have lived in a different one

One that consumes all life, life taker, not giver, played the piano keys abroad

Breathing in new life, filling the lungs with sweet melodies of the crisp air

I am now awake, awake for the day to come play about, for night has not
opened his eyes, for the time is yet to come

Beautiful day, where is thee? Why to run and hide? For we both make the
everlasting way!!

Your glory has yet to be fulfilled, such memoirs that one wants, but needs
to be complete

The sister moon is now awake, for the day has grown old, nothing left for
us to do, but once again to pay our due

**FOREVER ARE WE HERE TO STAY, ONCE AGAIN TO MAKE
THE VIVID DAY**

I SEE RIGHT THROUGH TO YOU

I see right through to you

I feel each, every move

To taste the breathless lips of passion

To smell the unfolding, strawberry breath

I hear the melodies of the golden,, untouchable death

Because you have it all, have it all

The very meaning of this foreign, lovely intent

The relationship, cause and effect of this true moment

The fountain of ecstasy that willingly awaits

To spring about, such passionate joy it creates

Because you have it all, have it all

EXPRESSIONS

I see your face, your eyes shine with no hesitation, such sparkling beauty lies inside

To live, is to grasp the innocent breath of your lips, so tender and moist

I can taste the sweetness of your homeland, wanting to forever stay

I traveled such far distances for you, a pilgrimage at best

I kiss thy virgin lips, sending a secret invitation to you

A pilgrimage, a journey through love, you and I will take

A field of hope, we have no boundaries, for faith is by our side

A dagger of hope, we both grasp so tightly, to stare into the face of thy enemy

For those who say it cannot be done, well, my friend, it has been done!

For all those who say it won't last, well, my friend, it has!

You complete me, as do I to you

What you fear is what I feel in you

Take my hand, as if I am riding the impending waves with you

For you and I are one, one being, one breath, one taste

As water, drip lets on the side, but as one, together, fullness

You blanket thy soul with your passion, as being as it may

You show the golden bridge, setting the path, its way

FAMILY TABLE

I sit at the table, waiting for the food to be ready

I ask my mother a question, for why do I always suffer from such intense anxiety?

My mother responds, I don't know, eat your food

I sit at the table, asking another question, why does one doubt ever so much, for is it but my fault?

Once again, my mother responds, I don't know, eat your food

The food now becomes cold

I sit at the table, and ask my mother one more question

Why do I doubt, everything that lay about?

For what is the very meaning of my illness??!!

I don't know, says the mother

THE FOOD NOW GETS THROWN AWAY

Mother responds, why do you have to ask so many questions?

Dinner, is now a memoir of the very past

INTRUSIVE MEMOIRS

I sit down and think, pondering cautiously about what we call life,

I fear that I have nothing to give, that temptation over rides thy self,

All that I have to fear, encompasses my heart, grasps my soul,

All that takes my breath away, seizing thy self to nakedness,

Pure in mind, innocent virgin of love, show me the golden bridge,

That transforms emotion into feeling, a feeling so divine,

In which there are no sweet tasting words to describe,

One who sings the sounds of the doves, to be immortal,

Life giving, not taking,

Oh what love smells of, so sweet, yet at times, so bitter

Night into day, day into night, a thousand souls walk hand to hand

High amongst the stars that dance, and flaunt their passion for one another

You give me life, forever as it may be, whole as water,

Drip lets apart, yet connecting body to body,

Forming thy self to be one again

One with thy self, one with the excited moon,

Shining its yellow brilliance, enlightening the spirit of the invisible storm,

So, So, calm, yet one can ride the peaceful waves, encompassed into a
blanket of youth

That in which directs the soul, into the unknown abyss of compassion,

May the wind be at your side, the sun towards your back, enlightening the
path that takes
you afar

In your quest, I say, to remember this,

That there are infinite songs in the bounty of life,

Pick the one that defines your emotional baggage,

And carry it to your one, and only destination of what may be

ONE TASTE, EVERLASTING

I sleep

I sleep in the blackened darkness that awaits thy self each and every moment

Though I am neither lost, nor afraid

For heaven blankets me, encompassing my body from head to toe

I sleep

Not knowing what direction is intended for, but with joyful intention to meet about

To meet ones self, a reflection of the past, for the mirrored reflection of ones self

A reflection of unconditional revelation of ones soul, stirring the wind like, blackened night

Stirring up the unforgettable memoirs that one had once lived through

A memoir of the past, now staring into the enlightened brilliance of the future to come

Of what may come, no one knows nor desires to know

For they have a belt of Hope and Christened faith to lead by their side

One can only taste the sorrow of yesterday, but the sweetness of tomorrow

Comes with full force, a calm storm of impending waves, that crash upon
thy self

Caressing and soothing the blazing fire of the soul, waiting and pondering
to be put out

For another day as come, an invitation to all, to what may come

The bitter foreclosure of today, the vivid colours that sit and lay, waiting
to grow new life

New hope, standing fast by thy side, waiting to be called upon, for service
of its duty

To serve thy master, of which is the rightful owner, to lead the golden path
of innocent

youth, waiting for its moment in time, to uprise and prevail

For one must thrust the aged, rusted sword into thy enemy of hate, which
its downfall of

what may be, can only be seen by with faith amongst your side, dangling
of unforgiving memoirs of its past,

One speak of thy so easily, yet they haunt the restless soul, night after
night, day after day

Bringing black stricken darkness to a hault, for the march is long but over

Ending the day with a virgin kiss of love to, thy hand, and to thy lips

Of which the invitation has been sent, waiting for thy unconditional reply
of ones self

In which to become reunited with ones touch, ones heart, ones invisible,
yet most colorful

spirit, on lifes infinite canvas

To forever draw the beauty of life, its experience in all

ONE TOUCH, ONE LOVE

RESTLESS SLEEP

I sleep

Sleep in the blackened darkness that awaits thy name, and thy sinful soul

Nor am I lost, but not found

Heaven blankets me

I sleep

Memoirs of the past stir about, with no sudden fault

Winds stirring, revelations abound

Sweetness of tomorrow, bitterness of today

Comes with full force, calming storm conveys impending waves, deep within

Blazing fire of my soul, for there are no limits here

Hope, stands as a marble statue, tall and erect

Ending the day with a virgin kiss of love, amongst thy tender hand, and soothing lips

To become reunited with ones touch, ones taste, ones love

An experience in all, this is what we call life!!

I SWIM

I swim into the dark, blackened abyss

I swim, with hope being at my side, breathing directions into my lungs

That even though I swim into the unknown, I can feel it inside me

Holding and caressing my fear, as if it just came out the womb

Of a mother so tender, so full of life, so that one does not know even the meaning of fear

Nor pity, for one does not even yet know how to pity

Each stroke, independent of each other, having their own meaning of truth

The waves crash, over and over, but yet I do not fall under their curse

For hope is still, at my side, forever being or afar

I must stay the course, and not stand fast, for then I will not reach my destination

The unknown destination that I crave and hunger for, the destination that in which I can

hear the melodies, but do not know the notes

I am so close, but yet, so far, for it seems so infinite, a dream per se?

No, no, for it is reality waiting to be taken a hold of

This is not fantasy, but yes, it is so vividly real

I can smell the tender, sweetness of youth, on the top of my tongue

And feels up my stomach with such a divine feeling, that one cannot even say

My only love from thy only hate, today is too soon, but tomorrow to late

AN EVEN PACE

I take one step of life at an even pace,

A pace that comforts my emotion, satisfies my hunger

Sweetens my taste, fuels my body, naked as it may be

For I am already clothed, clothed with your sensual beauty

A beauty that is hardly even known to man, a beauty that lies so deep

In thy self, that some might dig their whole life for, as if it weren't to be found

To the naked eye, one will not see, but close your eyes, and it may be

For pure, innocent loves that strikes with a bolt of lighting,

For it can not be seen, nor heard, but felt within the heart of one man

One that breathes air into the lungs that are drowned, without hope being
at its side

One that grasps the power deep within, which only eyes of the blind can see

Its brilliance radiates the layer of earth, in which its grass grows tall

With the moist-stricken air, that soothes and caresses, the growing of knowledge

One might say, that yes, we will live for tomorrow, and yes, the next day

From one end, comes a new beginning, a new beginning per se

For do not let life breathe for you, but in contrast, let it be you who
breathes life

For life will taste not the sorrow, but the joy of you, you who are so free

HEAR ME NOW

I walk the lonely life away, casting new memoirs of today

I walk the beaches of one so deep, digging in the sand so deep

I wish I wish, I could see your face, walking at an uneven pace

For you complete me, as you to I

From the golden heavens above, we soar so high

I taste your tender lips, kissing with ease

Never to stop, never to please

We swim together in the vast ocean of love

To taste the salt, from high above

Each stroke, independent of each other, I dearly love you

For me, as a brother, I stand amongst the might waves

Rolling and crashing about, never unsure

Without a staring doubt

I love you, to the very last breath,

Staring finally, into the vivid eyes of death

But where there is darkness, there is light, ever so bright

I now know why the caged bird sings, such melodies to hear

Just whisper my name, for I am always so near

CITY DWELLER

I walk through the vivid city, so full of life, parading about, without any
fault

Skyscrapers reaching towards the sky, secret window within, that lye

People amongst people, talking about, forever full of life, without a doubt

The crisp blue air, moving through our veins, the crisp blue air, together, it
rains

For this is where I live upon thee, to become a city dweller, this, is all me

Cars that pass, on the left and right, cars that speed, scribbling on the road,
able to carry passengers, such a heavy load

So the day is young, and the night is old, I become one, for life is never,
never done

Take my hand, and ride with me, lets get out of this concrete jungle,
together we flee

So here we are, once again, never to return, for the country is our new best
friend

I love thee, for you are the whole world for me

Together, together, we shine with glee

TURN OFF THE LIGHTS

In darkness, I see only but light

In darkness, I feel only but love

In darkness, I hear only such sweet melodies

In darkness, I taste only sweet innocence

In darkness, I smell only but the foreign fruits of the elders

In darkness, I walk the unknown path, which way it leads, one does not know

In darkness, I swim the currents that run through my cold veins

In darkness, I feel only but warmth, for I have tinted robes of faith

In darkness, I walk the thin cable of life, each step, independent of the other

In darkness, I convey only trust, in which truth sets thee free

In darkness, I am but one, one mind, one being, one soul

In darkness, I am set free, for I see only light

DARKNESS HAS NOTHING ON ME, FOR I AM EVER SO FREE

BLISS OF THEE

Journey

We walk alone this vivid night

You and I, we complete each other

One taste, One touch, One love

We breathe life into the dead, casting spells of love abound

The sun rises again, pouring it's brilliance upon all

To feel such warmth, only the inner heart can feel, such passion

The sandy shores of one thousand souls, stir in the middle of night

Shinning jeers to the sister moon, it sees all, feels, all, knows all

Playing amongst the golden elders, wisdom glimmers about

To love thyself, to love thy neighbors, for love conquers all

A shield of empathy, for I feel for you, as you to I

A dagger of trust, pierces through the blackened abyss

Conveying such light that hides in the darkness

For in darkness, there lays inner freedom

Night turns into day, casting the deceitful sorrows away

Soldiers of love, encased with robes of compassion, cast away evil that lays ahead, blocking the steps to the golden palace

Fighting to their last breath, scribbling freedom in the sky

FREE AT LAST, FREE AT LAST

EYES OF PERCEPTION

Last night I fell a sleep amongst the vivid yellow-glazed stars

I thought about death, it's purpose in all, how could such a thing ever so be

For what is the true meaning of life, when death is abound?

Why does such a wonderful world have to end in such a way?

So dark, like the blackened abyss, the depths of the deepest ocean, higher than the highest mountain

For I cannot see death, for I only see life

In darkness, I but see light, no such meaning puts forth to an end

Never in my life, have I felt so near to the thin red line, for this is all but new to me

How can something be so dark when one only but shines, such brilliance, such youth?

I now know why the caged bird sings, for it scribbles freedom amongst the naked clouds

To soar ever so high, to new levels of existence

Death? What is thy death?

For I only see life!!

ASHES TO ASHES, DUST TO DUST

A journey that takes one afar, to boundaries of no limits

Taking ones soul, drenching it in complete faith

As if it were a dagger, piercing the skin of youth

So innocent, yet so content, a mother's only child

Cries a thousand souls, bring noise to one's deaf ear

Walking the cable of string so thin, where to begin

Watching stars without you, my soul cries

Kissing thy tender lips, a pilgrimage through the depths of life

One can see the heavens of the white-dove clouds

Soaring ever so high, rain darting about, cleansing the sorrow sins away

Opening the cage, in which the very bird is set free

Singing sweet sounding melodies of innocence, flowing within our veins

As the wind, we flow through the currents, jeering shouts of joy

Together, you and I are as one, as the vast ocean about

Impending waves crash upon the shores of youth

Mixing the sands of the elders, bringing wisdom to one's mind

Letting go of the deceitful past, stirring vast memoirs of today

You and I, the baritone symphony we play

The jazz of life, through the trumpet of love

We dance amongst the stars, for there are no limits, an endless journey of ecstasy

UNBALANCED EQUATION

Fruits of life, grasps the life of one, first at roots, then to grow

One breath, one mind, one body, in all, total completeness

Revelations foreshadowing memoirs to come, to make thy day

Step by step, we grow, reunite to again be ever so free

Souls connecting, synapses sparking, chemical reactions taking place

We flow as currents through the crisp, blue water, such vast rivers

Balancing the equation of life, both the good and the bad

An experience to experience, life, isn't it grand!!

Such passion we have, for this is our day, our vivid day

Imprinting our feet into the sandy shores, we make up the sand castles

Logic, converting in to such passionate love, encompasses all to be

Such vast motive, purposeful to the very meaning of life

We, the people, planting the seeds of growth, watching as time passes us
by, let us not cry

Shedding our innocence, we become naked again, pure, virgin like

For you are what you love, not what loves you

To connect, only connect amongst the elders

ONE DAY WE WILL MEET AGAIN, BUT UNTIL THEN, GOODBYE
MY FRIEND

THE GOLDEN ELDERS

Life, what memoirs stir the day, casting deceitful sorrows away

All the things you said, running through my head

Just you and me, nobody else, so we can be free

Upon this day, this very moment, times has no bearing on us

For we scribble love amongst the glazed stars, and hence, behold them again

For true love dances amongst them, pouring into our veins, such a vast ocean they swim

Oh life, sandy shores, pebbles of infinite life, infinite boundaries that await us

Watching stars without you, my soul cries tears of sorrow

The very feather of life, floats upon the sky, hence, casting a spell of lust

They say that once you die, all your questions to life are answered

Well, in death, I only see but light, shinning ever so brightly

For their not gonna get us

Something so divine, one cannot see nor hear, but felt only within thy inner layering of one's soul

Brother sun, show us the way, to the golden palaces above

A game of chess the elder gods play

Each movement, independent, forever casting the storms that we ride

Through the vanilla heavens

Ah, how grand life can be!

My soul, bearing not deceit nor sorrow, but to be free!

A NEW PATH

Life, such a mighty grasp it has on me

Capturing my soul, being caged, never to set free

Of what may come, what may be?

I didn't ask for this life, so why me?

For higher than the highest mountain

Deeper than the deepest sea

I still cannot figure this out, maybe I should just pack my belongings and flee

Someone help me, hurry fast. Before I know

My life will pass, through the golden doors of heaven itself

I can't seem to finish this puzzle, for it just teases my mind

Maybe there is life after death, an understanding, in all, too divine

Where is thy brother sun, for sister moon has captured each day

My love, I think that this may be the end, wait, maybe a new beginning to an end

Yes, there it is, a solution to the death of my depression

Oh what pleasures life brings, setting forth a new path

LIFE GIVER

I lay on the dirt-stricken floor, shackled from head to toe

For life has a might grasp upon thee, a hundred fold

I stare into the deceitful abyss, in which direction do I lay?

Smelling the innocent strawberries of life, which encompasses thy soul,
blankets thy tender heart

To stare, without any doubt, proudly lifting my head up ever so high

My heart is cut into twp, one of pleasure, one of pain

To taste the bitter sweet blood, that swims through my cold veins

Hearing the silent symphony, marching of one thousand souls

An invitation, foreshadowing of what love to abide

A dinner of foreign fruits, to taste the unfolding beauty

Shinning through the fog of hate

To see the canvas of life, painted ever so brilliantly

For black and white has no meaning here

To be one again, as the ocean, riding the impending waves about

OCD

Life holds such intrusive thoughts

Impulses spark about, throughout my elaborate body

Neurons firing at the speed of light, connections being made

Thoughts that cast upon doubt,

No one is at fault, just something that comes about

Emotions that ride the impending waves of sorrow

Deceitful images that invade one's privacy

The smell of unfolding beauty, an infinite book of knowledge

One must come to terms with his sanity, becoming the person for which
who he is

ANOTHER DAY IN THE OBSESSIVE COMPULSIVE MIND

LITTLE STAR

Shinning its brilliance upon thee, sets the vivid day free

Little star, such light that shines amongst you, for you set the way

Little star, so earthly, becoming of age, growing older by day

Little star, shedding its innocence, such a spell it casts, of unconditional love

Little star, pouring its light, turning night into day, forever making the day

For you are the very meaning of life itself, such emotions that parade about

Little star, glowing from the high heavens above, where the virgin doves soar

Little star, as a new born child, you make life worth living for

Little star, you set the day, you show us the destination to where love subsides

No where to run, no where to hide, kiss life's tender lips, forever saying
goodbye

Little star, O little star, you grasp life from thy inner heart

Never to depart, how your presence makes your mark

On the vast sandy shores of freedom, imprinting your feet

Never to be washed away, turning black and white, into grey

Ah! The canvas of life, little star, will you be my wife?

GRASP THY LIGHT

Little star, you take my breath away

Little star, you turn night into day

Little star, how you know each and every direction, it's path, it's way

Little star, you take amongst the sun, the very meaning of light

Little star, how you only come out at night, to parade about

At no one's fault, being as it may, such truth you convey

For you shine light into darkness, light in the abyss, nothing to hide, nothing to miss

Little star, how you make each day, pouring out unfolding beauty

The smell of innocent roses, in blessed water they rest

Always stay ever so fresh, for new life springs about

For there is no night, but only day, night doesn't want to come out, not to play

Little star, you take my breath away

Turning black and white, to fuse, such a colour, grey

Little star, you paint art on the canvas of life, such vivid emotion

Never ending, so much devotion, so much spirit, for do not fear it, but

Hold dear it

LONELY NIGHT

Such a lonely night, we walk together, side by side

Holding hands, the mighty grasp of love between us

I stare into the glazed moon, pondering amongst the pitch black sky

A thousand souls stir in the night, chanting their whispers about

The wind, ah, so soft, soothing our skin from head to toe

The light of the moon, pouring its brilliance upon us, conveying the true meaning of life

Tasting the sweet innocence of the young night, for it is as a new born child

Sleeping in the womb of its tender mother

Life giver, you breathe into thy lungs, fulfilling thy hunger

Another lonely night, standing erect as a marble statue

Conveying mighty power from within, true confidence in all

Another lonely night, shedding it tears of hope

For today is a new day, new life springs about

To dance amongst the blackened abyss, ever so deep

To dance amongst the campfire, sending a secret invitation to all

We dance and dance the night away

TO FOERVER SEND NIGHT INTO DAY

LOVE

The greatest thing in life to love, and to be loved in return

Without love, there is no logic

After they had explored all the suns in the universe, and all the planets of
the suns, they

realized that there was no other life in the universe, and that they were
alone. And they

were very happy, because then they knew it was up to them to become all
the things they

had imagined they would find.

Lanford Wilson

It was a cold frigid day, the weather came with full force,

The heavens came down from above, sheltering ones being

It was a sheet of love, that encompassed all

One mind, one body, one soul

Together, anything was possible

To do anything

Be anything

To become one being divided amongst all

I stare into your face

Yours into mine

The sun is ours, together we shine

Turn night into day, day into night

To become one being, fullness, all encompassing

For the greatest thing in life is to love, and to be loved in return

True love dances amongst the stars, and is infinite, forever lasting, forever being

Eric Krueger

LOVE OF ALL LOVES

To smell such innocence in the air

To taste the foreign fruits of the elders

To listen to the baritone melodies of one's soul

To wear the robes of such vivid passion

A vast ocean of pure liquid brilliance, shinning through the darkened abyss

To touch the softened skin of one's unfolding beauty, in which never defies

To smell the love, flowing in the inner currents in which our lungs grasp

To live, to experience the limitless fields of fire, burning ever so deep

A brand new day, such lonely memoirs seem but to fade away

From the golden heavens above, raining tears of innocent youth

Spreading the fields, new life grows about, from the inner roots of life

To soar above the white dove clouds, through the pink-vanilla sky

To paint freedom on the canvas of life

To scribble hope in the vivid picture, conveying such love

In all, life, is all too divine

To play chess with the elders

Each move, independent of each other

Moving about around the wicked paths that are set about

To move with such vivid grace, true art at one's heart

Setting forth new life to spring about, for the memoirs of yesterday fade
away

For the fate today has not been decided, for it sends an invitation to all

To become one again, with the elements of pure ecstasy

One touch One taste One love

We will prevail, and set forth, new freedom

PARADING AMONGST THE MOON

Love

Is in thy air, our lungs consume such vivid fumes

Grasping for more, ah, it feels so good

Body tingling from head to toe, such currents, they flow

In thy cold veins, warming up the bitter-sweet pain

I love you, as you do to I

We soar ever so high, above the white dove clouds

Dancing amongst the sun, parading on the sister moon

Turning the radio of life, to our special tune

You and I, well, we grab life by our mighty hands

We run through infinite fields, such beautiful lands

I hold thy hands to the sky, resisting the urge to cry

Ah, life is so grand, I feel ever so high

Never to decease, never to die

We shout laughters of love to the stars

Forever, forever, they will be ours

Lets take this to the golden palace above

In that case, we fly from the gas of love

The greatest thing in life is to love and to be loved

LOVE BY MY SIDE

I see your face, your eyes shine about, no hesitation, unfolding beauty lays
beneath

To live, is to grasp the innocent breath of your tender lips

Sweetness comes to thy mouth, such a vivid taste!

I traveled such far distances to find you

Such a pilgrimage, for so ever far

Fields of hopes, have no boundaries upon us, we run raising our hands to
the sky

You complete me, as do I to you

Take my hand, as if we are riding the impending waves

For you and I are as one, as water

You blanket thy soul, ever so much warmth

The golden heavens above us, await our coming

FREE AT LAST

Love is now in thy air

Lungs consuming it's unfolding beauty

As a flower, it blossoms heavenly so

To become born again, free of sin

Love is now in thy air

Capturing all that was once free about

Encompassing the world at hand, such a mighty grasp

Blowing a tender kiss, it sets the virgin day ahead

Making all well, setting the cage bird free, singing such beautiful melodies

That lay deep within our softening skin, running through our veins

Never feeling hurt, never feeling pain, for this is our day

The very meaning of life, to love and to be loved

Scribbling freedom amongst the white-dove clouds

Painting such vivid colours on the canvas of life

Such a beautiful painting it is, such life it shows!!

Love is now in thy air, without any despair

To never depart, we two, we leave our innocent mark

On the vast sandy shores, with the tide at rest

Two imprints of feet, for this is our domain

The day is but young, and night has not awakened

Winds chanting dances of rain

To set the day free, of whom ever, to be free!!

MIDNIGHT

A thousand souls stir in the night

I hear their echoes, bouncing off the vanilla stricken walls

I hear the silent symphony, playing on and on

Their breath, and mine

Together, we intertwine

As one, fullness, all encompassing

Together, we are as water, such a vast ocean

We dance, and dance amongst the glazing stars

Forever lasting, forever being

MOON

Sister moon, come play with me, for I am ever so bored

Sister moon, come lay with me, for I am ever so bored

Sister moon, come dine with me, for I am ever so thirsty

Sister moon, have a glass of wine with me, for I am ever so thirsty

Sister moon, come walk with me, for I am ever so restless

Sister moon, come and talk to me, for I am ever so deaf

Sister moon, come talk to me, for there is nothing left

Sister moon, come soar with me, for I am ever so high

Sister moon, please adore me, for I love you ever so much

Sister moon, pour your brilliance over me

TO SET ME FREE, WHERE EVER YOU MAY BE

THE BAND KEEPS PLAYING ON

Music rings about, dancing on top of the white-glazed star

Perfection is made, new memoirs stir the day about, without a fault

Smokes a pack of poetry a day, downs it with a shot of beautiful melodies

That run about, to the open doors of the mountain

Higher than the highest mountain

Deeper than the deepest sea

The white feather of life, floats amongst the white dove clouds, for the very meaning of life is but upon us, darting down as freezing rain

Becoming one again, a transformation that may be, cleansing one's mind

All together, so divine, canvas of life, what do you paint for us

Pink vanilla sky, encompasses one's thought, so intrusive that it may be

For what is the meaning of life, does it have one, does it too have a soul like mine

Does it too breath in life as I do

Can anyone hear me, for I shout such sweet melodies, blankets thy naked body so cold

Sandy shores, imprint my feet, I too, can make a statement, confirming my life

Vast ocean, infinite boundaries, until the white-picket fence

Setting one ever so free, for this world, this moment, this error in time is
MINE

The caged bird is now set free

MUST ONE HAVE WINGS?

Must one have wings?

To soar so vividly in the sky?

To soar amongst the white-dove clouds, where the golden heavens await?

Must one have wings?

To visit the elders above, to play life's game of chess?

Life, so full of imagination, one can only think!

Of what dreams may come about, for there is no fault

Must it rain on this sunny day? Yes, it can, I say!

For we play, shedding our youth, setting the very way!

Our time has come, the day is yet but young, sister moon, where is thee?

Are you yet but still a sleep? Sister moon, why do you weep?

For we love thee just as the others, you, your innocence, is our mother's

Tender kiss to thy hand, singing the melodies of the bitter-sweet symphony band?

We few, we lovely few, we dance ever so high, no limits, no good-byes

LOVERS

Such beauty that lays under the vale

Take my hand, grasp the life that we have, for it is ours for the taking

Your eyes sparkle, as if they were fresh cut diamonds, pure, innocent

To hold you in my arms, to cuddle with such thee, blanket of
unconditional warmth

You make me feel like I am young again

Together, the journey begins, as we are about to start

Directions unknown, not to be seen, nor heard, but felt within thy heart

I hold your hand with a mighty grasp of hope, for it sits on the right hand
side

We must stay the course, always stay the course

Such a glorious day it will be, when we complete this pilgrimage

Thousands of connections made, one love to be felt

Always look ahead my love, and never look back

For the wind, whispering on our backs,

The sun, shinning the path to which leads us be

READY, SET, GO!

MY YOUTH

My youth ponders beneath the white glazed stars

Staring and gazing ever so gracefully

Revelations abound

The star shines its youth upon thee

Opens my eyes, sends a tingle down my spine

Encompasses my heart with love and joy

Someday to reunite with the elders, who once roamed this place we call
life

To hold hands again, to dance amongst the blazing campfire, singing and
praising ever so much

To become family again, brother and sister

To become innocent again, a new beginning to an old end

A new variable in the equation of life

Somewhere, some how, the answer lays

For it cannot be seen nor heard, but felt within thy soul

The silent symphony playing its vivid melodies amongst the sister moon

To know that each step brings us closer and closer

Waiting to swim in the vast ocean, a blanket of young purification

We will meet again, but until then,

Namaste my friend

NOT GONNA GET US

The love that casts between us

Lies too deep for one to see, nor hear

But can only be felt in thy inner layer of one's heart

Beating rhythms of passionate love, pumping through our cold veins

With a blanket of warmth, robes of empathy, cover thy body whole

Our bodies lie naked to the cleansed eye, opening an invitation to all

Come be one with us, for they do not hear us

Come be one with us, for you complete me, to be ever so free

To walk amongst the shores of tender youth, never to grow old

To run through the fields of infinite boundaries, gliding through the whispering wind

We are two of a kind, breathing in life from the fire

We dance amongst the stars, beholding them in our mighty grasp

We dance, moving the beats of the silent symphony, never to end

To live, ah, what life brings!!

MEMOIRS OF THE PAST

OCD= intrusive thoughts that enter one's mind

Thoughts that have no ending, for their purpose in all, is to live

To ridicule one's head, infinite boundaries lay in this blazing field

To jive and jeer one's sanity away, fulfilling the very meaning of its existence

To rant and rave, dancing amongst the insanity that is now about, pondering without

Any hesitation, for the moment lays ever so true, now understanding why sadness is blue

Tasting the bitter-sweet hour of darkness, not knowing in which directions lays ahead

For in this very darkness, there is no light, but only an abyss of one's deep thoughts

Intrusive thoughts shot by cannons of FEAR, now knowing the very meaning of life

For are we all not but stuffed animals, waiting to be plucked?

THIS IS WHY THE CAGED BIRD SINGS

WINTER SNOW

Once in winter, I fell a sleep, next to the vast ocean of white snow

As I awoke, something pressed softly against me

A deer it was, so young and innocent, as I stared into his eyes

I saw such beauty arise from him, though he seemed to be a little cold

I took my hand, rubbed his body, soothing the numbness away, for never
to stay

He looked at me, as if we were two peas in a pod, being one, together, all
encompassing

I gave a nod, as did he, and we both went on our way, such a day, such a
day

To this day, I have only to think of him, such amazement that unfolded

I now breathe in air of curiosity, for this is all that I have left, left to give

This day shall never be forgotten, for the very meaning of life, was at hand

These days will never be absent, for they stir the new memoirs of today

Leave the past behind, for the light of the future is to come, turn night into
day, forever we stay

For I have found a new brother in life, one never to forget

ONE SUMMER EVENING

I sit down near the edge of the lake, dabbling my feet above the water,
splashing about

Its ripples of innocence and youth soothe thy soul, my dearest friend

The reflection of the suns reflects upon the surface of the lake, leaving
behind a heaven scent view

A pink vanilla sky looms about, for day has wakened his eyes

The wind whispers amongst the vast lake

It welcomes all, comforting ones soul, as if it were a blanket of warmth

The day is young, night is but an old friend

The elements of earth communicate, as a daughter to her mother

Love is in the air, our lungs grasp the beauty

Connections that we have with life,

Oh, What a beautiful life it is

PHONY WRITERS

Phony writers, who do not write

Phony writers, who do not excite

Phony writers, listen to this, alright

You think you spit rhymes from time to time

Too bad, your writing should be a crime

You like to rant and rave with all the rest

Even though, its all but a stanky mess

I am not even going to rhyme for this

Its not worth my time

So go ahead with your sorry as rhyme, for it's a fool at best

All your scribble, is just a filthy mess

HOW SWEET IT IS

Playing chess with the elder gods

Bringing new wisdom, without a doubt

Shedding new light upon thee, making way to set free

Each move, independent of the other, sets forth new life to spring about

Ideas being born, memoirs being made, roots of youth are yet to come

Two minds, becoming one being, so divine in all

In a robe of tinted trust, one makes a move with no hesitation

Setting a new beginning to an old end, a path that leads into the unknown

But we have a dagger of faith upon our right hand side

To conquer sorrow and fear, to make haste a new day

One that spreads light into pitch black darkness

The dark abyss has no invitation here, for it deceitful lies are but memoirs
of yesterday

Walking the thin cable of life, balancing both good and evil

Each cautious step, conveying such truth in all

The very bird that sings the such sweet melodies above us, gives inspira-
tion to lead upon

For conveying the very meaning of life, how sweet it is!!

A vast ocean of empathy, loving all that breathe in the same air I do

Filling thy lungs, so full of unfolding compassion

Yes, my friend, this is life

HOW SWEET IT IS

POETS IN MOTION

Listen to the poets a wise man said

Hear their whispers, listen to the sounds of life as they pass you by

To tell you the very meaning of words

A purpose driven so deep inside, for it cannot be seen, nor heard, but felt
within thy inner heart

The poets lead the way, conveying such truth in one man's life

Expressing such love and compassion, one can only want ever so much

Words blanketing the soul of ten thousand souls, making friends with thy
enemies

Touching, kissing, becoming one

Listen to the poets, for they will lead the way, to the unknown path that
leads ahead

Show us the way, to reach the foreign fruits that await us

POETS, SUCH POETS, LEAD THE WAY

RAIN

The clouds cry, releasing its sorrows of the day,

The storms calming rain, soothes and caresses thy inner heart

Washing away the sins of yesterday, preparing to make way for tomorrow
to abide

The clouds are now cleansed, pure love shines about, making way for one
to be free again

The sky shines through the darkened clouds, breathing new life, for a
virgin day is here

One that is pure of heart, in which brings joy to thy inner layering of ones
soul

Freedom is now at bay, in which casts a spell aboard, happiness is now at
our side

A sword of light, turns night into day, shinning its brilliance upon all the
soldiers

The soldiers that are cleansed by the rains from the gods high above, and
armed with the

innocent swords of unconditional love

In which cannot be defeated, under no circumstances, for it is made by the
hands of god

The creator in all

We will walk in the valley of death, and shall not be afraid, for the enemy
is near

The one that casts spells of sorrow and hate, but forever is too late

We are armed from head to toe, with the sword grasped by thy mighty
hands of God

For the enemy is weak, and is cleansed by the rains above, for it is pure in
heart, in all too
divine

We have prevailed the battle between sorrow and hate

For it is all but an illusion, a merely date

For love is all but infinite, a friendly mate

I kneel down before my creator, and kiss thy hand

I open thy arms, with the intention with FREEDOM TO RAIN

RAINS THAT WILL NOT STOP

The clouds cry, releasing the sorrows of the day

The storms calming rain, soothes and caresses thy inner heart

Washing away the sins of yesterday, preparing to make way for tomorrow
to abide

Clouds are now cleansed, pure love shines about, making new way

Lonely sky, shines through the white-dove clouds, a virgin day is here

One that is pure of heart, inner layering of ones soul

Freedom is now at bay, casts a spell, faith is by our right hand side

Sword of light, turns night into day, unconditional love subsides

Creator in all, for we adore you

For you are pure of heart, in all, too divine

ONE HIGHER STEP

Shinning wisdom from high above the white dove clouds

Shedding forth the young days tears of comfort, blankets of heaven scent

To touch the soothing skin of the elder gods, making one's pilgrimage afar

Walking the sandy shores of innocence, impending waves of hope spread
amongst the beach

To swim in thy vast ocean of love, to feel such content, to feel such
passion, springing about new life, memoirs of yesterday seem but to fade
away

Soaring amongst the heavens above, becoming reunited with thy family,
feeing one's soul, hence, beholding the stars again

The very bird, that jeers melodies of one's escape, into pure ecstasy,
pondering about

To run the cornfields, spreading thy hands open, sending a secret invita-
tion to all

Setting forth a new, unknown path, in which one walks with such faith

A dagger of hope, piercing night into day, for in darkness, I see only light

We escape the darkened abyss, never to become captured

For we are one soul, protecting us with a belt of compassion, ever so
secure

For the world is in the grasp of our hands, never to let go

You and I, well, we hear the silent symphony playing such sweet melo-
dies, freedom rings about

For this is life, never one to be at fault, opening up the enclosed vault, in
which money has no value

For we share the same air, breathing in such joy, filling our lungs, setting
forth

Rhythms and rhymes skip at one's feet, to an ever life changing beat

LETS TAKE THID TO THE NEXT LEVEL MY FRIENDS

SILENT MIDNIGHT

The silent midnight speaks, playing its games in all

Whispering a high-pitched tone, a thousand souls hear it

Secret invitation for all to come and dance

Symphony plays of infinite hope, no boundaries, open fields of fire

Pleasure tingles down thy spine, pure ecstasy in all

Unfolding beauty, opens Pandora box,

Casting a spell on us, in a trance state, parading about

I take a deep breath, inhale the good, exhale the bad

To solve this vivid equation we call life

Beats and rhythms raving on and on

Can't stop the dancing, for it takes hold of you

Our destination unknown to the naked eye, for only the blind can see

The wind, by my right hand side, sun amongst thy shoulders

Leading the way to the golden palace

Truth now shows its face, brilliant in all

For there is only love between us, nothing more, nothing less

Grasp thy hand, you give me the need to proceed, for the doors are now open

HERE WE GO!!

RESTLESS YOUTH

I sleep in the dark, all alone, with nothing to hide

I am neither lost nor afraid, nothing stands in thy way

Which direction is which? One does not know!

Pondering amongst the past, new memoirs stir today

Revelations abound, the very meaning of life

Of what may come, no one knows!

A bitter taste of sorrow, with a spell of doubt cast about

The storm, so calm today, for it is at rest

New hope arises from the dead, giving back life

Innocent youth spread amongst the blazing corn fields

Ending the day with a virgin kiss

It wasn't all that bad, for I have survived

Another sleepless night, what dreams may come

QUESTIONS AMONGST TRUTH

Some say that all the questions to life are answered when you meet death

I think and feel that one needs to live

In order to find such answers, for isn't that the very meaning of life?

To love and to be loved!

Ah, How grand life can be!

Not to live, but to experience the foreign fruits of the day

To scribble freedom amongst the pale grey clouds

To add color to the black and white picture

To paint ever so vividly on the canvas of life

I see your true colors shinning through

The thick pink-vanilla sky, ever so high

Brother sun, show us the way, to the doors of the mountain

To the golden palaces above, where the elders set to rest

To play chess, as in life, each move, independent of each other

Striking fast at ones heart, parading amongst the campfire

On such this cold, lonely night, a vast ocean of darkness

For in this, I see only but light

For in death, I only but see life

The very feather that blows through the riptides of the day

Setting forth, a new way, to skip upon the pebbles of life

Shedding one's innocence, such youth cast aside

For true love is never to subside!!

SWIM

I swim

I swim into the dark, blackened abyss

I swim, with hope at my right hand side, breathing life into my lungs

I can feel the unknown inside of me

Just coming out of the mothers womb

A mother so tender in heart, for fear has no limits here

Waves crash, chanting thy name, sending an invitation

I must stay the course, stay the course damnit

Air in which I hunger for, is lost

Sweet melodies spring about, jeering sounds of a parade

I am so close, yet, so far away

Reality is in thy mighty grasp

Sweetness of unconditional youth, so infinite

Feeling so divine

Forever, forever you are but mine

A BRISK WALK

Taking a brisk walk in the park, one discovers many things

Such memoirs that are stirred about, as with no one's fault

Sun shinning with glee, until this day, now, free

Walking amongst the vast pond, one discovers such content

This is life, this is want is to be meant, scribbling freedom high amongst the sky

Soaring up and through the clouds, who said this day had to end, in which, why?

Why does this party have to end, for you are just beginning to be my friend!

Taking a brisk walk in the park, one discovers such truth, unfolding light

Turns night into day, a grasp of air filled with might

We are free, free to please, never wanting to leave

Cast thy troubles away, painting the black of life, into a vivid grey

Taking a brisk walk in the park, one truly defines himself

Life's true paradox

For in discovering life, one actually discovers himself, the greatest of all

A NEWBORN CHILD

The awakenings of yesterday prevail the memoirs of today

Casting the deceitful sorrows away, so that they never may stay

A new day is born from the womb of its mother, new hope, new life spring
about

Life giver, breathes upon all of us, conveying its whispering message

A secret invitation for all to come, to be with us on this such glorious day

The night is yet young, and day has not wakened its eyes, so we mustn't be
loud

For one to hear the bitter sweet symphony, its silence in all, encompasses
our golden

hearts
To taste the foreign fruit of the pilgrimage that one must travel ever so far

That one cannot see with the naked eye, but is felt within thy inner layer-
ing of the soul

That is infinite in its tender touch, in which blankets thy spirit, comforting
ones self

For there are three things that I must convey

ONE TOUCH, ONE TASTE ONE LOVE

THE BRIDGE

I sit and dangle my feet above the distant clear blue water

There is a bridge, that connects us both to this human earth

It is quite sturdy, with a warm personality to it

Though it is worn down, prevailing its past to us

I sit above the ripples, pondering about life, for what may come

It is calm, the water is relaxed, as a new born child, who sleeps in the arms
of his mother

To swim, amongst the water, would be freedom to ring

The protector of all above, gives the signal for the go ahead

Watching over as ones brother, keeping us from harms way

An experience of a life time, I too extend my arms to you

TO CONNECT

A NEW BIRTH

The day is so young, and night has not yet shown it's face

We sit amongst the vivid white stars, glazing such about, pouring it's brilliance amongst all

I can hear the whispering wind, talking ever so much, jeering about life, it's infinite touch

The sister moon, spills out her youth, casting a spell of a tender kiss

We walk amongst the vast shores of doubt, with a dagger of hope by our right hand side

Never to fear, never to give in, for we are angels at heart, beating always close, never to depart

I stand with so ever so tall, marking my domain, imprinting one's soul onto the sand

The silent symphony plays such sweet melodies, skipping into one's hand

My love for you will always remain the same, such soothing skin, calling my name

We soar above the white dove clouds, dancing amongst the lost crowds, of life per se

Never to stop, not this very day

Our love conquers all, the mighty world within thy grasp, free to be,
finally at last

LOVE ME, AS I TO YOU, FOR WE ARE SUCH A HAPPY FEW

SUCH EFFORTS WE DANCE

The effort of the un become to the becoming, such a constant effort

Such vivid drives that compel me, intrusive thoughts race about

One flower, one leaf of grass, for we are two peas in a pod, united, becoming
one

These words that I speak, for they are the very meaning of life

They flow as currents of the ocean, impending waves bringing them to shore

Imprinting them in the vast sandy shores of youth, waiting the unknown to
become the known

Giving birth to a each and every new day, scribbling freedom amongst the
white dove clouds

Suns setting in the distant north, night is but ready to show its face

As a canvas of life, we must now paint it black

Grasping for air, give me the need, to proceed, to the golden heavens above

ONE TASTE, ONE TOUCH, ONE LOVE

THE FIRST DANCE

I look into your face, watching your eyes glaze upon mine

Tasting virgin lips of sweet vivid innocence, sending my invitation

Extending my hand, waiting for the bride to be with me

To take our first dance, step by step, foot by foot

We mark this domain, for it is ours for the taking, imprinting our feet into the ground

Symphony plays melodies of love, pacing the room by the speed of light

The room is all but a blur, for I only see you, such beautiful you

We are as one, water, drip lets on the side, but one,

One taste, one touch, one love

Hands clapping, faces smiling, bodies parading about

Taking life by its hands, and blowing it as if it were a kiss

The night is ours, for the memoirs are still in the making

DANCE I SAY!!, DANCE!!

THE GOLDEN JOURNEY OF HOPE

A field of limitless possibilities

The grass grows in no boundaries, for it is free

In which one breathes a single breath of freedom, freedom to come

That forever carries the white feather of truth

A journey so far, not to delay, to makes its way

Across the vanilla sky, a canvas of life, insightful brilliance

An invitation to all, in what you fear, I feel in you

Take my hand, as if I am riding with you

Above the white dove clouds, ah, life, isn't it so grand!!

Destination cannot be see nor heard, but felt within thy inner heart

In which lays ever so deep, never asleep

We few, we battle night into day, making way, for others to follow

Forever being, nothing to fear

THE GREY ZONE

The baritone melodies of the train comes to a halt

The young doors of youth opens, conveying the deceitful message

An unknown invitation is sent out to all people

Step by step, we walk the gateway into the inner realms of death, how
wrong this feels

The symphony sings its vivid songs of sorrow, each step, awaiting our turn

The soil begins receding away, until pure, darkened dirt is but upon us

Each independent step, the conveying music becomes louder, more crisp in
all

The smell of human fumes feels thy lungs, consuming all the air that was
once so pure

The sky turns a burgundy pale, releasing the tart ashes of ones soul

The chalky, smell of death is but upon us now, its gases consumes our
bodies

Are we all but just stuffed animals, waiting to be plucked?

Our voices transform into distant echoes, bouncing off the bathroom walls

The stultifying fumes are now released, making our lungs breathless

Our insecurity and fears await, opening up pandoras box

Our vision becomes distorted, our bodies tremble

Our hearing becomes distorted, leaving one almost deaf

The insipid gases are now vented

Our bodies are carried by several foreign souls

For ashes to ashes, dust to dust

Lord, have mercy on those who doubt, for it isn't but their fault

NEVER FORGOTTEN

JAZZ IT UP

The jazz of life, for it to be, the very message, to set one free

I sit amongst the crowd, ever so loud, jeering on the artists to play abound

Such sweet melodies, that the song conveys, that of love, for it sets the way

So here we are, again at last, together, together, do we ever fast

From the foreign grapes of youth, ah, how sweet they are

To soar above the white dove clouds, however measured or afar

So take my hand, and dance with me, for the golden gods set us free

To be with me, one being, thee, lets take this to the next level

Where love shines with glee

Your body, mine, against each other, in all, too divine

Our hearts beat together, to be so, intertwined

We dance amongst the heavenly sky, ever so high, together, together, must we ever die??!!

NEVER TO BE FORGOTTEN

The longing for that one last touch

That one last tender kiss

That one last special hug

That one last sound of your innocent voice

That last smell of your bitter-sweet perfume

That last sight of your eyes, glaring amongst the sun, ever so heavenly

The last taste of your mouth, as if the sun were amongst my tongue

THAT ONE LAST MEMIOR OF YOU

ELABORATE ONE

The meaning of death

Let the pain be

And death, where is thy death?

Where is it, where can it be?

There was no fear because there was no death

He turned his attention to it

Well, what of it? Where does it lay?

In place of death, there was light

What joy it may be!

It is now finished

The man stopped in the midst of a sigh

Stretched his whole elaborate body, and then died

ONE HEART, NEVER TO DEPART

The moon, the sister of the sun

So dark, yet so bright, it conveys truth in one

I am lost, but the moon is still by my side, forever being

It leads the knowledge of youth, into the destination of age

As if one matures, each step, independent of the other, taking on the baggage of ones soul

Running into an infinite field, a field of layers upon layers of ones spirit

For the inner truth is nor shallow, but deep, in which one can dig and dig,

But what is to be dug? What does it convey?

In this, I ask you in what direction must you may

For the truth is already shown, in being so gay

In essence, the vivid colours paint the day

I say to you this, that there is only love between you and I

Far above the white dove clouds, the never ending sky

We fly so close to the heavens far above

As we are traveling on the outskirts, of innocent virgin love

I blanket thee, with thy most inner heart

So that two transform into one,

That we never depart

LEAP OF FAITH

The pond amongst the yellow painted cabin

Showing such life, currents and ripples send their messages

Not to delay, the becoming of such a day, sweet melodies played about

Trees swaying left to right, spreading its innocence, soaring ever so high

Grass pondering about, spreading unfolding beauty into the air

The smell of woods, the smell of such vivid life, the effort to become

The longing for that one last run through the naked forest

Raising thy hands in the air, blowing an invitation for God to come

Come to play about, for there are no faults!!

AN EXPERIENCE

The purpose to life, one may never know

But I must convey three things in order to live and survive

You must be able to do three things:

TO LOVE
TO BE LOVED
TO KNOW WHEN TO LET LOVE GO

For this is the very meaning of life

One must understand the depths of the darkened abyss

The depths in which can drown thee, stealing away one's soul

One must understand the notes to life itself, it's beautiful melodies in all

The piano of life, such tunes it conveys

For death has no value here, it is but a word, a simple word

For in death, I only see life, new life that springs about, from the stems and roots of the secret garden

For in darkness, I see only but light, a simple light, that forever shines, it's brilliance in all

For the past is the past, the future is the future, but now, is the moment in which I am alive, to live, to experience

EVERLASTING LIGHT

The silent midnight, playing its games and all

Speaks to one, with a whispering tone to his voice

Speaking the dictionary of a thousand souls

One by one, they send out their secret invitation

For all to come, for all to hear, the symphony of infinite hope

To hear the symphony, and its soothing melodies

That caresses thy soul with its sweet, tender touch of love

Pleasure run downs my spine, giving me a scent of freedom to come

I smell the unfolding beauty of the new midnight

It casts a spell on me, for to be one, thee

I take a deep breath, for all of life tragedies to come forth

And then exhale, for toady is a new day, a new beginning to a distant end

Ones own sins are now set free, free amongst the white dove clouds, where
they dance

and dance, and forever going on

For I too hear the beats and rhythms playing through my mind

So many there are, for which one to choose, however measured or far
away

I take each step, independent of each other, climbing into the night, for it
shows me the way

The wind, by my side, the sun, amongst my shoulders, the light, shinning
forth in front of

I

For I now see the steps, of the golden cast bridge

The destination, unknown to the naked eye

For it cannot be seen, nor heard, but felt within thy heart

My soul, cries out, waiting to be heard, waiting to be comforted

In thy warm encompassing blanket of truth, that covers me so deep

It's now time for me to leave this world behind, for it too is a distant
memoir

For there is one thing that I must convey to thee

There is only love between us, infinite, unconditionally

So, now is the moment so near, I kneel down before you

Kissing thy virgin hand, and one sweet tender kiss to thy lips

Let us be on our way, for the golden heavens await our beings

It's time to go, grasp thy hand, and proceed through the iron cast doors, for they are now

open, sending its invitation of innocent love to come

SONGS OF HEAVEN

There are many songs playing in my head

Which one to pick, which one to choose

Which one leads the way, the golden cast bridge

I feel the wind brush softly against my soul, smothering it with content
comfort

A warm blanket of many kinds, kindles me to be one and divine

I taste the sun, amongst my tongue, the sweet and bitterness of life as it
may be

I look into your star stricken eyes, and I see life, many hopes to come

Take my hand, grasp the breath of mine, the sweet tasting kiss on to your lips

I feel the invitation of love, see the glory of your youth, whispering to my name

I smell your unfolding beauty, seizing me from head to toe, nowhere to go

But to cast myself amongst the innocence of your soothing motherland

A place of unconditional simmering light, turns night into day, always
leads the way

One touch, one taste, one LOVE

THE MEANING OF IT ALL

There are many things that we cannot explain. One of them is the mystery of life. What is the true meaning of it. One must question the true reality of things. Even though it can seem so complex, it is actually very simple. Live in the moment, enjoy the moment, and take pleasure in what you are doing. The greatest thing in life is to love, and to be loved. That is the truth of it. If one thinks too hard, then you loose the true sight of it's content. Every single God given day I wonder what is the purpose. In my experience, the best thing to do sometimes is not to think, but to live. That is what love is truly about. I have never really experienced love, but from what I heard, it is truly worth it. I hope that one day, I will be able to experience it. At the moment, I am done thinking about what life is about. I am just going to live it, and enjoy it to the fullest Life at times can get too complicated, then in which one gets too confused about the true meaning. Though, what kind of God one make one suffer so much? I always have to question this? Life can be so unfair at times, and I wish that this just would not be. People say that one has to suffer to know what true meaning is, but I do not understand this. I think that life should be about enjoying it and being able to be happy and love. I guess you could say that one has to see light in the pitch black darkness. Maybe that is the truth of that. And in essence, there really is no darkness, but in which how one looks at things from their perception. Things sometimes I guess you could say just do not make sense. They say that when you die all the questions to life are answered. In some aspect, I think that his has a point. But, one can still answer the question also while being alive. The most complex question leads to the most simplest answer. To love and to be loved. That is the main point. Every single day of my life, I have to deal with obsessions and intrusive thoughts. I can never understand what the true meaning of them are. Maybe they are nothing but bulllshit. Though, then again, maybe they are some sort of purpose that was given to me. Who knows, but I am the one who cares! I want to be able to enjoy life to the fullest, enjoy happiness, to know the true meaning of love. So far, in this life, I have not experienced one of them. And it is getting to the pint where everyday is just the same. One day after another, hour after hour, minute aft minute. How many days is it going to take before I can actually enjoy life. To wake up, to see the sun shinning, to listen to the birds sing their beautiful melodies. This is what I crave for, I hunger for this. It is my addiction should I say. I love writing to you because you always listen, and share the same feelings that I do. Writing is one of the best things that I ever picked up. Everyday I will write to you, conveying my innermost thoughts and feelings. Then I can reflect on them, and in essence, grow to a better person. For I need to grow, everyone needs to grow, that is the journey of life. Everyday we understand a little bit more and more, and learn new things about one's self, the infinite limits of the pure mind. Life is like a ever growing class, taking new notes each and every day. The teacher, in essence, is really our selves. We are the creators in all. We lead the way for thy self and others. There is no such thing as a stupid question either. Every thought has an action. Our thoughts are who we are. They tell us the truth about things. They tell us what is right and what is wrong. They tell us what is ethical and what our morals should be. Like I said before, thoughts are what makes us human. After thought, then comes feeling. After feeling, then comes behaviour. This is what we all must learn, and try to grow and stem from. Dear God, have pity on those who doubt, for it is not their fault, but only being human at mind. That is what makes us human. Faith is something so hard to grasp, I think and feel that it is the hardest thing to believe in. There is so much hate that goes on in this world, one can almost doubt so easily. But, I guess that is what faith is all about, to believe in something that one cannot see or hear. In essence, faith is something that we have to believe in but in hwhich our senses deny. I hope one day to learn the truth about life. This will be such a glorious day. Maybe I already know the truth, but just do not see it, or believe it. Yes, life is such a mystery, one can only dream of what it means. I think that there are hidden clues all around us, in which if we pay close enough attention, you can actually see. But why are there such hated in this planet? Why are there so many wars going on? This is something that I will never understand. Maybe we are not suppose to understand, maybe that is the truth of it. In which we do not understand, then, we must have faith. And faith leads us to each and every new day. A new beginning to an old end. AH, yes, I am finally understanding this now. One must not think so hard, and just enjoy the moment. Live in the moment! Love thy moment! This my friends, is the true essence of life itself, and hopefully, we can all achieve this. Writing will always be my greatest friend of all. I will never let it out of my sight. I have been writing for about two years now, and I still cannot get enough out of it. I am always excited to feel my fingers tap the keyboard of life. Such a thrill it is, to visually see and feel what you are doing! Yes, writing is my best friend, and I am here to tell all, and to convey the message to all. The greatest thing in life is to love and to be loved in return!

HEAVEN

There once was a door that lead to the mountains

They say that it was covered in gold

Inside lied the keys to heaven

Such a place, such a place

A thousand souls stirred in that place

Such vivid memoirs that were spared

Such a place that one never hears of

There once was a door that lead to the mountains

They say that inside were the foreign fruits of life

If eaten, they say you could live a thousand lives, over and over

They say that it was a place of the elders, a place that was of conversation

Many vivid conversations jeered about in here

Mostly about life, it's purpose and meaning in all

Such a lovely place, for heaven now had a name

And this is where the people went on there pilgrimage to the next life

There once was a door that lead to the mountains, I must not forget, but it's name was

HEAVEN

PAINTED CANVAS

There seems to be many out there who think poetry rhymes

What do I think, Well, it is more then just rhymes

Poetry is something that has to come from the heart, not just putting
rhymes to rhymes

That's something that a child can do, for there is more to it then just that

Poetry takes skill, talent, and a special gift with the swaying of the pen

Poetry is a skill that can take years to master, for some may say that it is an
ever lasting

journey, with infinite boundaries,

Poetry is to have words paint the canvas of life, with each and every true
colour

For you must convey the passion, and drive, in which one feels

How can you describe truth in rhymes???

This is something that a kid does, not a true poet.

A true poet uses words as his dagger, and his thick covered shield to
surpass his opponent

One must use his word as a chess player moves the pieces of life onto the
next square

So all you rhymes out there, in essence, be aware

FOR I SEE YOUR TRUE COLOURS SHINING THROUGH

IΝFIΝIT€ FI€LΦS

They ran through the fields of ice, such passion they carried

Running ever so vividly, spreading hands up in thy air, as if praying to the elder gods

For it was ever so cold out, blood running through our veins

Wearing a tinted robe of happiness, sorrow had no place in such a village

They say that it was so cold out, they no one would ever live in such temperatures

But true love was at hand, performing it's daily task, warming thy inner layering of one's heart

Filling our lungs with such compassion, one was never too cold, for there was unconditional warmth sitting by our right hand side

We were soldiers of the day, setting forth the ongoing way, to the golden palaces, such a pilgrimage for one's feet

But in fear, there was only but love, and in hate, there was only but joy

Higher than the highest mountain, deeper than the deepest sea

Once again, we are caged birds, set ever so free

POETRY SMOKER

They said that he smoked a pack of poetry a day

And drank a glance of wine to wash it down

Such brilliance that it was, such shinning light, on this cloud-stricken day

For brother sun has made his first appearance, sister moon sleeping during the day

Foreshadowing many storms to ride the glazed night

To be one again, as the water, drip lets on the side, but one, fullness, everlasting

For the day is young, casting deceitful sorrows away, fulfilling what may

For we dance amongst the stars, and hence, behold them again

For this is our day, our moment in time, history in the making

Imprinting our lives on the vast ocean sandy shores

I kiss thy lips, ever so pure

Cleansing thy soul, becoming whole again, your heart, mine

Together, we intertwine, hence, in all

Much too divine, for we jeer upon this moment in time

Casting a spell, ever so bright, bringing on new memoirs that stir the day

For we are so free, free to be, ANYTHING

The caged bird, the very soul meaning of life, is now set free

Freedom rings, freedom rings!!

SILENT LIGHTS

They say she smokes poetry for breakfast

Eats short stories for lunch

Eat novels for dinner

They say that words run through her veins

As if a vast ocean of thought, intrusive thoughts parade about

Collection of unfolding beauty, brilliance pours about

They say she has a collection of books

Of one that contains a thousand souls, stirring in the night

They say that all she does is read, and then, read some more

They say that she is a scholar, one that knows all

People come from every direction to see her, for her wisdom is ever so true

I once took a pilgrimage to see her, and she told me the truth

And the truth was: **In darkness, there is only light**

THE CURE

They say that a touch of love cures all

They say that a touch of love heals the soul, unfolding beauty comes about,

Without a doubt, without any hesitation, loves cures the lonely heart

They say that love cures the blind, in which only the blind can then see

TRUTH, SUCH TRUTH,

A vast ocean, of which conveys life as it always been, a robe of shinning love

That warms the body from the elements of the darting rain, cleansing the
elaborate self

They say that love cures the deaf, in which they can only hear such
beautiful melodies that are played about

In which we dance and dance, amongst the campfires of innocence,
shedding our bodies

Becoming one with thy neighbor, grasping the infinite sky above, above
the white dove clouds

They say that love cures the numb, bringing new life about, spreading love
down thy spine, creating such vivid happiness, in which one parades about

They say that love cures the sad, filling the empty with such content,
unleashing beautiful shouts of ecstasy

They say that without love there is no logic, no meaning, for love is the
cure to all

THE GREATEST THING IN LIFE IS TO LOVE AND TO BE LOVED

A LOVELY PLACE

They say that all your questions to life are answered when you die

I say that all your questions are answered when you truly begin to live

This is the very meaning of life, this is why the caged bird sings

Life giver, nor taker, you breathe in me life, it's youthfulness in all

The very existence of mankind, such vivid purpose

For all humanity, we take each stride closer and closer, to the doors in the mountain

That's were the elders stay, their home in all

Some say that this place has a name, from the foreign fruits of the long pilgrimage at hand

Heaven is thy name, such a holy place

A place where the birds soar above the white dove clouds

A place where the symphony plays such beautiful melodies

Melodies that soother thy naked ear

Men wearing robes of tinted passion,

Little star, how you make such a day!!

Little star, you breathe in me life, life to dance amongst you, infinite
boundaries in all

You make me feel so young again, as if children parading about, with no
fault

Heaven is thy name, such a holy place

THIS SHIP OF MINE

This ship of mine, belongs to me, travels of the world

Bringing life to a stop, for this is our very moment

This is our time, our time to grasp the world, and blow ever such a kiss

Sandy shores, we imprint our feet amongst the shallow water, bringing the very definition of hope

For you and I, we are two peas in a pod, you complete me, as I to you

I kiss thy tender lips, setting forth a pilgrimage, such infinite boundaries

There will be no white flag above my door, for surrender has no meaning here

Listen! Can you hear? The caged bird sings such sweet melodies, tunes of life

They say that we both smoke poetry, and wash it down with a glass of melodies

Your heart, mine, together, we intertwine

Becoming one, as water, forever blanketing one's spirit

Such warmth you bring, deceitful sorrows subside

A realm of inner peace, ah, how grand life can be!

I know I'm not perfect, but I can smile

I'm no angel, but I still have wings

Scribbling love amongst the yellow glazed stars

Brother sun, show us the way to the open doors of thy mountain

Be one with us, forever so true, canvas of life, such vivid blue you paint

Colours of life, black and white have no meaning in this moment of time

The world moves at a steady pace, always at the touch of our hands

FOR THIS IS OUR TIME, OUR VERY MEANING OF LIFE

SNOWING IN THY MIND

Tiny drifts of snowflakes fall swiftly amongst the sky

Tiny specs of heaven shed their tears of joy

Blanketing the ground, covering a layer of pure white

Heaven now lies amongst the ground, an invitation to all

Such beauty is around us, many pleasures to come

Children spreading their innocence, mothers and fathers, they smile with glee

Snowballs flying in ever direction, for the children are parading about

Marching in tiny packs of four, treading amongst the snow, how beautiful
it is!!

Voices calling, such sweet melodies that drift through the air, sound waves
of pleasure

Oh My! What a day it is!!

Hopes and dreams foreshadowing brilliant memoirs to come

For this is heaven on earth!!

TO CAST A THOUSAND DOUBTS OF LOVE

To love and to be loved in return

Such mysteries life brings, new hope springs about

Confirming one's soul, stirring the impending memoirs

To dance amongst the stars, and hence, to behold them once again

We move about, to the melodies of life's silent symphony

To taste the foreign fruits of the elder gods

To walk the invisible road, taking one ever so afar

To the steps leading into the golden palace above the white dove clouds

To speak of such beautiful peace, such wisdom in all

To become one again, with the mighty universe, a vast ocean of darkness

For are we not but tiny stars in this world of such vivid love

Impending waves caresses thy inner spirit

Laying to rest the deceitful sorrows, for today is a new day, a new beginning

From an old end, walking the shores of such youth, never to become old

Tasting the innocence of thy tender lips

To run through the fields of youthful grass, spreading one's hands about

Toward the golden heavens above

AH LIFE!! HOW SWEET IT IS

TO KNOW THYSELF

Who am I?

For who are you?

Do we share our innocence together, as being one?

Do we not share the same texture of guilt that lay hidden beneath thy inner soul?

Are we all but naked, conveying an invitation to all

Do you swim the vast ocean of empathy that I do?

Do you not swim the rough currents of sorrow?

Where there is courage, I find nothing but doubt

Deafly listening, I hear your name whispered about

It calls thyself, casting a spell on one's youth

The very bird, struggles to become free

Free but unable, it lays content, in the jaded grass

Finally surrendering, it now accedes mortality

For the imprisonment is now lifted above, to the golden gods

The unanswered question now has it's solution

This is mortality

This is love

TO LOVE AND TO BE LOVED

Life is a journey, for the memoirs of yesterday fade away

What does this convey?

Each step, independent of each other, battles truth and honesty

To swim in the deep-pitch black abyss, waiting on deceitful sorrows

Embarking on an infinite journey, for there are no limits here

Through the thick, green, bladed grass, so pure of youth, for we stand
together, united, one

We open our eyes to the heavenly skies above, blowing a sweet virgin
kiss, to send the invitation

Innocent freedom runs down our spines, the very meaning of life

For life is to love and be loved in return,

Without this, there is no logic

So breathe life, and breathe it with full content

TO OBSESS

Ponder

To think

Mind overload =
intrusive thought that cannot be stopped
Intense anxiety, overwhelming to ones elaborate soul
Ones success turned to ones failure
Such unfolding pain one must suffer
In darkness, there seems to be no light
Higher than the highest mountain, deeper then the deepest sea,
for where are we

confusion of the vivid senses
No such control, one must be denied
Where to go? Where to hide? When will this spell subside=
Try to take control, try to control thoughts, nothing seems=
to work, for are we just robots? Where is thy purpose=
where is thy meaning?

I NOW KNOW WHY THE CAGE BIRD SINGS

TO SEE YOU, IS TO SEE HEAVEN ITSELF

Your beauty unfolds into pure ecstasy

Your body stands as a marble statue, to be seen and enjoyed about

To stand next to you, holding hands with thy mighty grasp, never to let go

For we hold the very meaning of truth in our palms, to blow a kiss and let
it flow

I love you with all my tender heart, such brilliance pours out of your soul

Whenever I am lost, I think of you and know where to go

To jeer melodies, with the wind, there they blow

Darkness subsides about, but together we glow

I walk with you into the unknown path, which directions I do not know

But we together, as so, always know thy love to go

I kiss thy liquid lips, flowing as water to be

Your heart, intertwined with mine, sets me free

For I love you more then the world itself

My greatest discovery, the love of your wealth

THE BOND

To take a rest next to a golden bridge

To take comfort in knowing that all is well

To feel content with thyself, ever to be so true

To know that all good things come in time

To feel secure in the womb of the mother, never to let go

To feel empathy for others, knowing that they too are human beings

To know that whatever lies ahead, we shall make it through it, both the thick and thin

For we are complete, one being in all, one mind, in all, too divine

We shall cross the vast ocean of tears, walking amongst the crisp vivid blue water

For time has no spell on us, forever we are so free, free as to be

As the wind whispers and blows, so do we ride the currents, to the golden heavens above

You and I, we can take on the whole world, for it lies in the palm of one's hand

Dear lover, take me afar, take me to the plains of infinite joy, spreading thy hands up to the sky, a feeling ever so high

FOR TRUE LOVE DANCES AMONGST THE STARS AND IS INFINIT, FOREVER LASTING, FOREVER BEING

TO THY LOVE

He stayed cushioned upon her, breathless, dazed, confused

With his heart beating like a hammer

One hand clasped her head, her lips inviting a single kiss

The other hand stroked her shoulders in a passion of love

He stayed cushioned upon her, with his soul encased in blankets of pleasure

For now the thunder was distant and passing away

The rain beating softly upon us all, casting a new spell

For love is now in thy air

INFINITE FIELDS OF FIRE

Today I sit, cuddling so

Listening to the silent sounds coming from within

Such thoughts provoke vivid emotions

Behavior responds, for first there is thought, then, there is action

Today I sit, wondering how the day will be

Foreshadowing events, and true colors shinning about

The day seems young, but casts a spell of infinite boundaries

To do so, by purpose of reason, to love thee, always

Doors waiting to be opened, for I have the very key to unlock Pandora's box

Setting free such pure brilliance, one can only imagine

The vivid mind, no hesitation at all, intrusive thoughts race round and round

To become one again

Free, for I now know why the cage bird sings

I NOW SET THEE FREE

BELIEVE IN ME NOW

Today I want to die

Today I cry and cry

Lost hopes carry me afar

Lost dreams lead me into the wrong direction, which way to go,? Which way to hide?

For I am forever lost, this world, so ever does confuse me

Senses are dazzled, irritated by intrusive thoughts

Brought on by the soul of anxiety, grasping the very life out of me

I am not worthy of your love God, for I have failed so miserably

I have to where to go anymore, please forgive me for my actions

Foreshadowing death to come, this is where I am from

Please forgive my doubt, for which it is not my fault

I am not me, but trapped inside a vast ocean of hate, in which consumes all

Life giver, I do not even deserve this life, for I am but a mistake

My whole life, such a puppet show, so fake,

I ache and ache

I shall meet death with my eyes wide open

For there is no love in I

NOW IT'S TIME, TO SAY GOODBYE

THREE KINGS

Upon the table, three kings sit

One laughs, one shouts, one cries

For the intrusive thoughts that come about

Pondering through the vivid minds, restless as can be

The one who laughs, laughs at the one who cries

The one who shouts, shouts at the one who laughs

Such common grounds that lay here, for no one is at guilt

Three kings sit amongst a table

One is happy, one is sad, one is confused

The happy king wonders why such a sad king, while the third king is ever such confused

What lays ahead amongst them, one will never know

Three kings sit at a table, such vivid emotions conveyed, pouring innocence into thy crowd, an audience per se

FOR THIS IS THE DAY, THAT WE CONVEY

VANILLA SKY

The moist sky, prevailing the golden gods from above

Speaks the symphony of truth. In which it conveys

Raining its 12;00 burgundy sorrows away

For it is time to come out and play, soak our deceitful sins away

The day is but young, night has yet to come

The lonely beach conveys such truth, an invitation for all to taste the foreign fruits

Casting a spell of joy, how grand life can be

Though loneliness sets in, for I am all but myself

What is there to do? Where to go?

Such a lonely day, I must convey!!

HAVE IT ALL

Watching stars without you, my soul cries

For you are the one who casts a spell on thy heart

So tender, so full of life, life giver, you take me ever so far

Your breath, intertwined with mine, completes me, forever making me
whole

For we are now one being, one life, one in the world of love

I love you, and will always love you, as the first day we met, you stole my
heart away

Your face shines with a thousand stars, glazing amongst the universe,
bringing light into day

We are forever young, restless as can be, we pace the world a thousand
times, and then do it again

I step ahead, leading the way for us, setting new life about, imprinting our
feet, marking our territory

This is our world, our world for the taking, for it revolves around us,
gravity keeps us from flying away

We shout melodies of freedom, to do anything, be anything

Fly anywhere, to the golden palace that awaits us, to sit on the right hand
side of God

What you have for me is different from the rest of us

Because you have it all

Have it all

WHAT I KNOW, MAY NOT BE MUCH, BUT TO THIS BE EVER SO TRUE

What I know, may not be much, but to this be ever so true

I love you, with all my heart and soul

Your tender kiss, subsides beneath my restless spirit

Your glazing eyes, sparkle upon me as if you were a lighthouse during the middle of a storm

Casting the way, to post dock at bay

You and you alone, complete me, as I to you

Intertwine, so divine we are, just the two of us

Grasping the world upon thy mighty hands, forever blowing a kiss

Sending an invitation of sweet melodies to flow about

Through the riptides and currents of life, the very feather that casts a spell upon all

For true love dances amongst the stars and is infinite, forever lasting, forever being

The caged bird is now set free, free to be, free to soar amongst the white dove-clouds

Shedding both innocence and youth, creating new life, a new beginning to an old end

Sister moon, show us the way, shine your unfolding beauty upon thy naked bodies

Comfort us in time of need, blanket us in time of sorrow

For you are the very meaning of life, to love and to be loved

The time is now, lets us be on our way!!

WHO AM I?

Do I know you?

Do you breathe in life as I do?

Do you hear the silent symphony too?

It calls thy name, fulfills thy heart

Do you walk the invisible road?

Do you take the same path as I do?

Do you taste the innocent strawberries of life?

In which it renders your soul, blankets the body, clears the mind

Unconditional warmth

Do you swim in the vast ocean as I do?

Shields of compassion, inner feelings of empathy

ONE DAY, MY FRIEND, WE WILL MEET

PLANET LOVE

Who made this world that we live in?

Who made the sweet-filling air that we breathe in?

Who made the vast oceans of water that carry the current of life?

Do you know?

I sit down and think, what are we, what is thy purpose?

Life, thousands of answers to the very meaning of why

Life, one thousand questions to the very meaning of thy answer

For the true purpose is not to question, but to experience!!

To love, and to be loved

For love is the key to thy golden palace high above, where the elders stay

Without love, there is no logic, hence, no meaning

For the past is the past, and the future is the future, but for now,

We live in thy moment about, without any doubt, you and I,

We dance amongst the stars, and hence, we came forth to behold them again!!

WILL WORK FOR HAPPINNESS

As I write this, I am trying to the best as I relay my ideas and thoughts on this piece. I don't know how good my mind and thinking are, but like I said, I will try my very best on this paper. I, as a little child, had this illness all along, but never knew what and how to cope with this. That dreadful feeling of impending doom, that feeling of intense panic, in which I thought that it would never go away. And to this day, I still have to deal with this beast, but I know now how to cope with it. And that makes life a little easier on the mind, body and soul. The clinical term for this is OCD, or in regular terms, obsessive compulsive disorder. Just the sound of this term sends shivers done my bones, and it probably always will.

I want to start back as early ad grade school. The reasoning behind this is plain and very simple. This is when the illness began and took its place in my life. Back in the day, my brother and I were switching schools from left to right. Mainly because my brother was having behavior troubles with the teachers. The funny thing about this or the irony is that I was also have troubles, but they were invisible to my parents, and I also kept them inside. It was about 8th grade when I really started to notice these transformations in which I had no clue what they were about at all. What was happening inside my mind was an abstract painting taking place. It was of confusion and chaos, and I had no clue what so ever on how to cope with these obscene, intrusive thoughts.

School for me back then came decently easy and was manageable, at least for a while it was. The ocd illness started to effect my school work and I at about the 8th grade period. I was starting to perform mind rituals, compulsions, and was getting intrusive thoughts non-stop during class time. I was now starting to have a difficult time even listening and paying attention to what the teachers were saying. My school work started to deteriorate, and my grades were also dropping as fast as b-17 bombers.

One thing that I noticed also was how my mood was. Everyday I seemed to have uncontrollable anxiety, which effected my thought process and behaviors. Things weren't as enjoyable as before, and it was now even hard just to drag myself out of bed in the morning. It seemed so hopeless to me, and I was having a hard time finding a reason even to live. That's when things started getting really intense. Yes, I would go to school, play sports, and do work, but it just didn't feel the same anymore. Doing normal day things seemed as if they were chores to me, as if they were things that I had to unwillingly do.Even my relationships with my friends started to roll downhill. Everything was just an abstract mess, and I was right dab in the middle of it.

As time went by, I eventually did finish highschool along with my other classmates. This was a surprise even to me, considering all the obsessions and compulsions that I was dealing with. I think the main reason that I finished was because this was just the onset of the illness, and it hadn't reached its full peak until beginning of freshman year. So, in essence, I was fairly lucky and time was on my side. During the summer of graduation, things only progressed worse. I now was probably spending about three to four hours a day on my thinking rituals, and I also had compulsions in which they consisted of working out for at least three hours a day. And even when I did these compulsions, I never had gotten the right feeling anyways, which made it even more difficult.

In the beginning of freshman year, I had joined the football team. All summer long, I had trained with fierce intensity which was intended for I to get a starting position on the football team. I have to admit that it wasn't even

183

enjoyable working out and getting in shape for the season. It was now just an compulsion, and intense urge that propelled me to do the things that I did. And to top it off, I had intense anxiety each and every day which haunted me nonstop. Things just seemed to get worse and worse, and soon along the spectrum, sometime or somewhere, a nervous breakdown was definitely going to happen. It was almost if it were destined to.

Football season finally came to an end, and this was a huge relief to me. All during the season I had been obsessing, performing secret rituals, and dealing with anxiety up to my hips. This, as with any human being, was not enjoyable one bit. It was as if it were a giant storm that had endless power to keep stirring up the night. One might say that the storm may never end, but its how one copes with it. I had no clue that I even had an illness, and therefore I was I ever suppose to know even how to deal with it. After football season was over with, I had about one week before wrestling started.

All the coaches were excited about the new freshmans coming in. There was a lot of competition in this class of people, how could one not be excited. I have to say that I much very so preferred wrestling over football, but maybe this was because I didn't obsess as much as football season. I mean, how could one obsess when there was not time at all to. Wrestling took time and concentration, and one had to fully devote their self to it in order to stay at par with the competition. Everyday we practiced moves, takedowns, throws, etc…If I were to obsess during this time, then how was I suppose to learn all the moves? So, in essence, this was sort of a distraction for me getting away from my illness. Soon enough, the meets came right around the corner. I have to say that I was so nervous before them, each and every one. But I did it, and I actually one a lot of my meets too. The final result would be earning a medal, in which one could most definitely hold their heads up high and proud.

We also wrestled in tournaments too. At first, for some odd reason I liked them. But as I soon found out, they took up way too much time. The whole weekend was shot, and you hardly had any time to even concentrate on your homework. This started to be a big time consumer, and I have to admit that it was getting really annoying. Every weekend was getting filled with wrestling tournaments, in which were all day events. To top if off, the coaches of the team were always making comments about me as if I wasn't putting forth one hundred percent effort. This was totally untrue which has some irony in it because I was one of the only athletes actually winning the majority of the meets. A lot of the things that they said I took personally, but maybe they were just joking around, this I will never know.

During the meets, one could wrestle once, and then have to wait several hours before you wrestled again. This in essence, became very tiresome and boring. One would hardly have enough energy to keep going. It became very stressful even on its own, not to mention the obsessions and compulsions. Wrestling had started to take its toll one the body both physically and mentally. During the middle of the season, I had already had enough of the tiresome sport. And like I said before, the coaches kept pushing and pushing to ones mental limits. Could this indeed be really worth all the effort? To my knowledge, I really think not.

Finally, over several months of the gruesome sport, it came to an end. Again, I was open with joy and happiness. It had turned out to be just if not more stressful than football. Everyday my mind would be obsessing on intrusive, irrational, silly thoughts. They would just bombard my mind as if it were fort Sumter during the civil war. Each time that one came into my mind, my anger grew more and more. I had no clue to what was happening to me, and I hated it so much that I felt as if I were going to explode. Like I said before, I had no idea that I had this illness, and to top it off, how to manage in coping skills with it.

After wrestling came to a hault, I had about a week before track started. I must say that I was very weary on if I should join or not. Each sport that I had accomplished involved much stress, too much stress for one being to live with. Sports were supposed to be fun and enjoyable, and in which this was the total opposite. It was if I did an 180 degree spin off of it. Instead of it being something pleasurable, it was discomforting and a pain. A pain that would never go away, something that stayed with you all along, throbbing its soul on to you. One could hardly live with this, not to mention even bearing with it. Yes, life was should I say very difficult for me, in which every day was a pain in the ass. You would think that things would have to get better sometime, but this was indeed false, and they only got worse.

As track started, everyone was filled with excitement and joy, except for me. I knew that it was going to be another long, difficult journey ahead of me. For every sport that I had played in the past was, and history I knew was doomed to repeat its self. The practices began without any hesitation, and the kids were running out and about. Things at first seemed maybe a little better, but this soon was short lived.

WINTER'S TRUTH—BEHOLD

Have you ever seen something more beautiful than heaven's white snow?

Have you ever wondered what does this convey?

Have you ever seen such warm blankets encompassing one's soul?

I too, have seen

I too, have wondered

Snow flakes from the golden heavens above, shedding such youth and innocence

Amongst the soldiers of the lonely night, setting forth a new path

A path that only the blind can see, with thy naked eye

The snow keeps on falling, flake after perfect flake, consuming all the brilliance of the day

Such lonely white fields, for they hunger for such vivid love

Love that cures all, for without it, aren't we but nothing, a darkened abyss?

For winter fills us with ever so much joy, joy that's warm thy inner layering of one's heart

Winter is abound, such truth it conveys!!

WORDS, WHAT LIFE THEY BRING

A man once said, what words you convey:

For they are the true essence of life, the memoirs of today

Each letter, introduced into an elaborate word, such meaning at bay

Creating an everlasting feeling, in all, much too divine

For the symphony plays, to set the beautiful, glistening day

To taste the sweetness of love, in which the mouth pours words that ever
so lay

In one mind, one being, words that scribble freedom, a universe of un-
touched hay

Pounding each mystic sound, in an area too grey

Ah! To smell the evergreen scent, of such unfolding beauty, the band plays
without dismay

A man once said what words you convey

LETS TAKE IT HIGHER, ABOVE THE CLOUDS, SUBSIDING AN-
OTHER LOVELY DAY

WRITERS

Acrobats of poets, pacing their own way

Treading on high voltage wires of their own making

For they set forth the unknown path, making way for all to come

A sea of many faces, salted, in such vivid colors

Beauty waits upon them, waiting for the invitation of one

Taking each step, independently, toward the lucid sky above

One discovers truth, the meaning of hope, to become one again

STAGE ACT

Yes, I do push my poems, so what, is this an internal sin?

I do it in the name of life, truth, passion, an ideals

Yes, I do push my poems, again is this an internal sin?

I do it in the name of poetry, in thy art so true

So how can one writer make you feel so blue?

Dammit, I a human being too!

You think you spit mad rhymes, Okay, maybe from time to time

But this poem is the inner layering of something too divine

Maybe you shouldn't cast down all the poets per se

It's a lame, insulting thought, that I must convey

So what you do is ur own insightful business

As I finish this piece, I hope that you didn't wish this

To be too personal, that I can dish this

So, all in all, I hope you weren't putting on a act

So all in all, that's why your receiving this flak

YOUTH HAD HIS DAYS

Lonely youth pondering beneath the stars

How sad the night seems to be, staring ever so gracefully

Revelations abound, unfolding beauty awaits

Opening my eyes to this new world, I see only but light

For dark is yet to be born, and shall it wait

Holding hands, walking the path, becoming who we are

Personality developing into the very meaning of human beings

To become family again, amongst the elders, playing games of chess

New variables in the equation of life, somewhere, somehow the answer
lays deep

Listening to the symphony playing its sweet melodies, dancing amongst
the campfires

Birds chirping away in the white-dove clouds, soaring so high

Life, what an experience to experience

Isn't life, but so grand!

Printed in the United States
116314LV00001B/74/A